Endomorph Diet

The Ultimate Weight Loss Guide for Women and Men with the Endomorph Body Type

Includes Delicious Recipes, a Meal Plan, Exercises, and Strategic Intermittent Fasting Tips

Contents

Introduction

Somatotypes is a term coined by William Herbert Sheldon, a doctor, and psychologist. His study of nude postural photos (not pornography, mind you) taken at some of the United States' most prestigious schools from the 1890s to the 1960s became the cornerstone of somatotyping –the process of identifying or classifying people according to their somatotypes. This system was shaped by Sheldon's studies and anthropometry exposure and the belief that body type can form part of a holistic and integrated approach to good physical, mental, and even spiritual health.

In the 1930s, Sheldon started synthesizing his somatotyping process. During this time, the terms *ecto*, *endo*, and *meso* became known to the general public. Before the Second World War, eugenics was one of the most talked-about subjects, and Sheldon was an academic "rock star." It didn't hurt that famous English novelist Aldous Huxley indirectly promoted Sheldon's somatotyping system. In his articles, he would often ask his readers, "What morph of man is your husband?"

Amy's Endomorph Story

Amy is a person that fits the description "big-boned" perfectly. What does this mean? Though neither fat nor obese while growing up, she wasn't that thin either compared to many of her friends.

Until her teenage years, her body fat levels never became an issue. It seemed that she didn't get fat, regardless of what she ate, but things changed during her twenties.

As she advanced in age, she discovered a concerning trend. Gone were the days when weight gain – particularly body fat – was merely a figment of her imagination. From her twenties to her thirties, it became clear she no longer enjoyed a carefree, no-repercussions diet. Adipose tissue (connective fat tissue between skin and muscle and covering some organs) started accumulating quickly, even if her diet was relatively clean and healthy. It wasn't perfect, but it was not unhealthy enough for most people to pile on the unwanted pounds.

So, what did Amy's diet look like? To start her day, she would typically eat what was considered a healthy, standard American diet (SAD): cereals, orange juice, and peanut butter toast. The typical fare consisting of a sandwich using green leafy veggies, meat, and cheese was her lunch. For dinner, she'd have protein (meat or fish) with a starchy carb.

She was also careful not to go too long between meals and increase her chances of binge-eating. That's why she'd eat mid-morning and afternoon snacks to keep her blood sugar – and consequently, energy levels – from crashing. Hence, she ate a handful of almonds for snacks.

She liked ending her day in a relaxed mood. That's why she had a glass or two of wine. Which, in her mind, also helped boost her health because of the antioxidant content of the beverage.

When you look at her diet, it doesn't look bad, right? I mean, she ate what the media had been promoting for decades as the breakfast of champions: i.e., cereals, fruit juice, and peanut butter sandwiches. She ate relatively healthy foods for lunch and dinner, i.e., whole foods and just the right amount. The same applied to her snacks.

But still, Amy kept on piling on the unwanted pounds. Why? For one, her lifestyle changed starting in her early twenties when she started working. From that point forward, gone were the days when she got sufficient physical activity on most days. As an office worker, sitting for hours on end every day became the story of her life five days a week. It also didn't help that her somatotype is – you guessed it – endomorph. As such, she easily gained body fat around the waist, thighs, and hips, just as weeds grow without care in most gardens.

What compounded her situation is that her skinny childhood friends continued being thin as adults! And they're mostly office workers with relatively sedentary lifestyles, too. Worse, their diets are not as healthy as hers. As a result, Amy feels that the world, universe, fate, or God isn't fair. In her heart, she asks why her – and not somebody else?

Fortunately, Amy isn't a pushover. While she would feel and act like a victim often, such moments were short-lived. Her innate personality compelled her to quickly get out of a rut and look for ways to change her status quo. That's why she persevered in getting to the root cause of her weight gain problem. With enough research, she learned about somatotypes and, more importantly, what hers was. You already guessed it right; she's an endomorph.

As she learned about the key characteristics of her somatotype, she felt a great sense of freedom! Indeed, the truth sets people free. In Amy's case, knowing the reason she quickly gained weight, despite exercising a lot of self-discipline and willpower, enabled her to finally lose that excess weight – and she learned how to *keep it off.*

You can do it, too, helped by this book. But more importantly, you can do it in a healthy, consistent, and sustainable way. Within these pages, you'll learn all there is to learn to start losing excess weight, keep it off, and achieve much better health. This book is packed with life-changing and practical information to help you start losing all that excess weight and keep it off for good. It includes foundational principles to practical ideas, including easy-to-prepare and mouthwatering recipes. In the end, you'll be able to live the fullest and most satisfying life possible because great health is *true wealth*!

So, if you're ready to start your exciting weight-loss journey, turn the page, and let's begin!

Chapter 1: The Skinny on Weight Loss

When you hear the term "weight loss," what comes to mind? Correct me if I'm wrong, but chances are, you're probably thinking of losing body fat or getting leaner. After all, our clothes don't fit comfortably anymore because of too much fat in all the "wrong" places.

This is where most people get it wrong. They suppose that simply by losing weight, they automatically lose body fat. This belief keeps many people from effectively losing weight and keeping it off, regardless of their somatotype.

Adding to that, there are many foolish ways people try to lose weight, thinking it's automatically about lowering the numbers on the scale. Some of these include exercising with sauna suits: the quickest way to lose weight is by dehydrating one's body, but it's an unhealthy way of doing it. Given that it's very easy to lose weight through dehydration, the flip side is true: it's very easy to gain it back!

The principle behind this is to make a person sweat excessively and, in the process, lose weight quickly. An even more reckless idea is not drinking water while preventing the supposedly lost weight from coming back.

This represents an unhealthy way of trying to lose weight regardless of the somatotype. Dehydration is one of the worst things that can happen to a person's body – even while at rest. Can you imagine how much worse it would be to continue exercising in a dehydrated state?

Regular exercise is one of the best ways to lose weight and keep it off. Intensity and duration are essential to successfully shedding excess weight. Dehydration, among other things, will significantly hamper your ability to exercise at the right intensity and for the needed length of time. Why do you think professional athletes gulp sports drinks like Gatorade and Powerade during games?

The worst that can also happen with persistently exercising in a dehydrated state is organ failure. When that happens, it's game over.

Extreme crash diets severely restrict caloric intake to lose the most weight in the shortest possible time. And while some diets don't do this, they can still be considered crash diets because they severely limit or eliminate specific types of macronutrients or food groups (the most popular is restricting carbs). They are impractical and go against the human body's natural mechanisms, requiring too much of a person's limited willpower reserves. And just like meteors entering the Earth's atmosphere, most people who go through crash diets eventually crash and burn. In the end, they don't just burn out but regain the weight that they lost and even more.

I'm not saying that crash diets fail *all the time*. However, a person's chances of successfully and healthily losing weight and keeping it off are very slim because of the reasons stated earlier.

Macronutrient assumptions: We will talk about macronutrients in more detail later. For now, know that they refer to the three main kinds of calories - carbohydrates, protein, and dietary fats. Everything you eat and drink that has calories contains at least one of these three.

By macronutrient assumptions, we mean applying the same ratios to everybody with the same weight goals. As you will learn later, one key to successfully losing weight and keeping it off as an endomorph will hinge significantly on macronutrient ratios.

Different Kinds of Weight Loss

The saying "A rose by any other name smells just as sweet" doesn't apply to losing weight. Why?

When you lose weight, it can be in the form of water, body fat, or muscle mass. The true goal of any weight loss program is specifically *body fat loss.* While it is practically impossible to lose weight purely in terms of body fat, you can ensure that most of the loss is the right kind of weight loss. You can still go down several notches in clothing sizes without losing weight, or you may even gain a few pounds. How's that possible?

Again, let's go back to the fundamental goal of losing weight, which is body fat loss. If your clothes no longer fit you, the chances are high that it's because of accumulated body fat. However, if you lose body fat and build muscle along the way, it's possible to fit into your old clothes while maintaining your body weight or even slightly increasing it.

To understand how this is possible, consider that muscle cells are denser compared to fat in terms of volume. Body fat tissue has a density of 0.03 oz per 0.03 fl oz, while muscle tissue has a density of 0.04 oz per 0.03 fl oz. To put it in layman's terms, if you lose 41 ounces of body fat but gain 31 fl oz of muscle tissue during the same period, you may still weigh the same. However, your waistline and general body size will shrink. It's because, in terms of volume, it takes less muscle volume to achieve the same weight compared to body fat. You may still weigh the same in this example, but in terms of tissue volume, you would have lost more fat tissue (41 fl oz) than you've gained in muscle mass (31 fl oz). Now, can you see the importance of ensuring that you lose mostly body fat instead of water and muscle mass?

Another reason you can weigh the same but look leaner is because of the way muscles and body fat determine how your body looks. If you gain 10 pounds of body fat, you'll look bigger, softer, and more out of shape. Contrast that to gaining 10 pounds of muscle mass. Doing so makes you look much fitter, leaner, and toned.

Another reason to ensure that you lose mostly body fat and minimal muscle mass is your metabolism. Between the two, muscles are the more metabolically active cells in your body. Having more muscle mass can increase your resting metabolic rate, which means you can burn more calories (and, consequently, body fat) even while physically resting. If you lose more muscle mass than body fat, your metabolism will slow down and make it even more difficult to burn calories and lose weight.

Also, having excess body fat levels significantly increases your health risks. Obesity puts you at risk for life-threatening conditions such as heart attack, hypertension, liver cirrhosis, and diabetes, to name a few. It also increases your chances of physical injuries because the excess weight puts too much chronic strain on your joints and muscles.

You see, losing weight can be a worthy goal, but it shouldn't be your primary priority. The most important benefit of losing excess weight is optimal health and wellness. What's the point of looking fit if you're unhealthy? Case in point: a triathlete friend of mine.

John is a high-level official in one of the biggest firms in the country. What's even more impressive is that he is a triathlete. The last time I saw him, he was very fit and buff. I even complimented him, saying I'd never seen him that ripped before. I never imagined seeing him this physically fit and conditioned, considering the nature of his job.

About two weeks after that chance meeting with John, I learned that he suffered a mild stroke. That baffled me; he was in incredible shape when I last saw him! Later, I found out that his blood chemistry, particularly his cholesterol levels, were through the roof, creating a blockage in one of his major blood vessels and leading to a minor stroke. Fortunately, it was just a minor one. After a few months of rest, therapy, and adjusting his diet, he recovered fully. Now, he isn't just physically fit – he is also *healthy.*

Therefore, when relating to a person's overall condition, we use the terms health and fitness. We can be healthy but not fit or be fit and unhealthy, the latter being the case with my friend John.

Now, I hope that your paradigm about losing excess weight has changed. If done right, losing weight can lead to automatic improvements in health. You will learn how to lose weight healthily and sustainably as an endomorph for the rest of the book. You won't just look much better, but you'll also be much healthier.

The Pitfall of Comparisons

Comparing your body weight and measurements while trying to shed off excess body fat can be a double-edged sword. That is why it's also essential to learn the proper way to compare your progress.

Why should you compare? Unless you do this correctly, you won't be able to track or monitor your weight loss progress properly. Comparison entails evaluating your weight and measurements using two specific benchmarks. The benchmark you use for comparison will determine whether you're comparing your numbers correctly or incorrectly.

You must compare your current numbers to your previous ones. Put simply, compare your current body weight to how much you weighed the week before. By doing so, you'll know whether you have lost or gained weight during the week.

Now, there's an incorrect way to compare your weight, and you must know this to avoid comparison pitfalls and maximize your chances of successfully shedding excess fat.

Never compare your body weight and measurements with those of others. That is a definite recipe for discouragement, false hope, and failure. Why is that?

Your body composition, genetics, personal circumstances, and history differ from mine and everybody else's. All these factors (and more) have a say when it comes to how fast or slow you'll be able to lose body fat and the strategies and tactics required to keep them off. So, comparing your weight loss development to professional fitness competitors is neither realistic nor practical.

For one, fitness competitors make a living from their physical fitness and conditioning. Their day job entails exercising and following strict diets all day, every day. These aren't side projects or hobbies – these are their *livelihoods*. As such, they can dedicate all their time and resources to exercising and dieting in ways that most people may find extreme or impractical.

As a result, they can achieve such high physical fitness levels and low body fat much faster. Also, it's much easier for them to maintain how they look. If you are not a professional fitness competitor, it will take you more time to lose excess body fat. If you compare your progress with such people, you will never measure up. It's a guaranteed recipe for discouragement and, eventually, quitting.

Another thing to consider when making the proper comparisons is circumstances. Weigh yourself and take body measurements at the same set time of the day and under the same set of circumstances.

For example, you may choose to measure yourself first thing in the morning every Monday before eating or drinking anything and after you have been to the bathroom. When you weigh yourself in this way, the number you will get may be considered your *clean body weight*, i.e., weight from food and drinks will not be counted.

But if you weigh yourself every week at different times of the day, you won't be able to compare apples to apples. Now, suppose you weighed 190 pounds last Monday morning (after going to the bathroom but before eating and drinking anything), and then weighed 193 pounds *this* Monday evening. You'd think that you had gained more pounds over the week despite dieting and exercising. If you believe this, you may adjust your diet and exercise to burn more body fat in ways that may become unproductive – or unhealthy.

For example, you may severely cut your calories even further and exercise longer, harder, and more frequently for the rest of the week – overdoing things and severely affecting your long-term weight loss success.

In this example, your body weight last Monday morning is considered your clean body weight. Most pounds/ounces represent your absolute weight, i.e., the weight of food and drinks were not counted.

But your body weight this Monday evening includes the food and drinks you've consumed throughout the day, less the ones you've excreted already. That means part of your body weight isn't yours but comes from the things you've consumed throughout the day.

You can't say you've gained weight when there's a high possibility that the additional pounds were not absolute body weight. Thus, it's important to weigh yourself at the same time of the day and under the same set of circumstances. Suppose you weigh yourself first thing in the morning (after going to the bathroom, but before drinking or eating anything), and your weight has increased. In that case, you've probably gained weight.

More than just weighing yourself, you must also measure your body fat levels because the goal here is to shed excess body fat and not just bodyweight for the sake of weighing less. Remember, if you lose more body fat than muscle in terms of volume, you may still look thinner or leaner while gaining a pound or two. This is possible because muscles have a higher density than body fat; thus, gaining more muscle can help you look fitter and leaner.

By taking both body weight and body fat level measurements, you can determine if you're losing the right weight, i.e., body fat. If you lost three pounds last week, but your body fat levels went up from 23% to 25%, that's not a good indicator. It means the weight you lost is either water weight or, worse, muscle mass. Suppose it *is* muscle mass, and the trend continues. There, your metabolism will eventually slow down, and the chances of you losing more weight and keeping it off decreases.

There are many ways to measure body fat levels, but there's usually a tradeoff between high accuracy and cost. The most accurate way of measuring body fat levels involves using highly specialized scanning equipment that may cost you at least $100 a pop. If you plan to monitor your body fat levels weekly, you may lose more than just body weight; your bank account may also get leaner!

The cheapest way to measure body fat is by using body fat calipers. Before the invention of sophisticated body fat measuring equipment, this was the gold standard. It was the only standard. The challenge of this relatively cheap and easy method is the difficulty in its use. It requires pinching different areas of your body – several of which are pretty tricky to do yourself – and measuring the thickness of the skin folds. Electronic body fat measuring equipment proved to be much more accurate.

So, the choice appears to be either breaking the bank or settling for a cheap (but difficult to use) method to measure body fat. Fortunately, there's another option. Today, it's easy to buy affordable and relatively accurate equipment that uses electrical impedance to do the job. These include digital weighing scales with body fat analyzers or handheld electronic devices that do the same thing. Between the two, you may want to choose the digital scale with a built-in body fat analyzer because you can weigh yourself and measure body fat in just one go.

Whether using a digital body fat analyzer, calipers, or a costly testing service, *consistency* matters most. Like the need to weigh yourself at the same time of day and under the same conditions, the accuracy of your progress tracking requires you to use the same piece of body fat level measuring equipment each time. You must track the increases or decreases in your body fat level consistently. If you use a caliper to measure body fat levels this week, then use a digital weighing scale that uses electrical impedance next week, it's pretty much like measuring your waistline using the metric system today and inches later.

Body fat numbers that decrease and increase because you're using different measuring devices are neither accurate nor comparable. If you use a digital weighing scale or a handheld body fat analyzer, you must be consistent in terms of the time of day and circumstances under which you use it. This is because your body's hydration levels can significantly influence the readings you'll get from this equipment. For the most accurate readings possible, measure your body fat level first thing in the morning, after you go to the bathroom, and before drinking or eating. That way, the readings that you'll get will be comparable and consistent.

It's All About You

Before we proceed any further in your endomorph diet journey, always keep in mind that it's all about you. Compare your results, or lack thereof, only to your last numbers and not anybody else's. You are not other people, and other people are not you, so don't expect yourself to progress at the same pace as others. Keep your eye on the prize and, more importantly, on your weight and fat loss developments. Your health and fitness goals are yours alone, and nobody should tell you otherwise.

Chapter 2: So, You're an Endomorph. What Does It Mean?

While this is a book about losing weight healthily and effectively, what sets it apart from other books is emphasizing a specific somatotype. It's about helping endomorphs succeed in shedding excess pounds. However, to better understand and apply the information you'll learn throughout this book, we can't skip discussions on somatotypes altogether. Are you an endomorph, or is your somatotype something else? Whether or not you already have an idea, let's look at somatotypes.

Endomorphs, Ectomorphs, and Mesomorphs

Somatotype refers to a person's physique type and body shape. This term is used as a specific system of classifying people's physical shapes developed by an American psychologist named William Sheldon. According to the system, there are three extreme body types under which people can be classified: endomorphic, mesomorphic, and ectomorphic.

A person's somatotype is typically expressed as a three-digit number. The first digit refers to a person's endomorphy, the second digit relates to their mesomorphy, and the last number is related to ectomorphy. Each number lies between one and seven, with one being the lowest and seven the highest.

For example, a person who is an extreme endomorph would have the number 711. The 1st digit reflects extreme endomorphy (7), and the other two reflect minimal mesomorphy and ectomorphy. An extreme ectomorph, on the other hand, will likely reflect the number 117.

Remember that extreme numbers like these are practically nonexistent or, at the very least, scarce. In effect, no person is exclusively endo, ecto, or mesomorph. What somatotyping is trying to identify is the degree to which people's bodies lean more toward specific somatotypes. Just as no one is entirely extroverted or introverted, specific somatotypes are not more dominant for any one person. As an endomorph, it simply means that your physique's primary characteristics mostly resemble those of an endomorph, and to a certain extent, contain mesomorphic and ectomorphic properties.

But more than just the general shape of the body, your somatotype also describes your physical, genetic predisposition, among which is your body fat levels. For this reason, you'll need to diet and train in specific ways compatible with maximizing your ability to shed body fat and keep it off in the long run. So, let's look at each somatotype in more detail.

Ectomorph

People with this somatotype are generally blessed with a fast metabolism. Their bodies can burn more calories even while at rest compared to meso and endomorphs. They also have a slight build.

Because of their generally smaller size and faster than average metabolism, ectomorphs find it hard to gain weight regardless of body fat or muscle mass. If you have a friend or family member who eats like a horse but is as slim or lean as a pole, you're looking at an ectomorph. An excellent example of ectomorphs is marathon runners, i.e., slight builds, relatively ripped bodies, and minimal muscle mass. Ectomorphs also tend to have narrow shoulder blades and flat chests. They're also naturally lean.

Because of their generally small frames, relatively lightweight, and low body fat percentage compared to muscle mass, ectomorphs tend to be ideal in speed and endurance sports. Again, look no further than marathon runners and track and field athletes. It will be hard to sprint fast if you're not optimally lean. To jump as high or as long as possible, which is the case in events like the high jump, pole vault, and long jump, you must be the lightest possible version of yourself. A 10-pound increase in body weight can spell the difference between winning the gold medal and not qualifying at all.

But because of their relatively light weight, ectomorphs aren't ideal athletes for combat and weightlifting events. This is because their relatively fast metabolism means they have less than average muscle mass, which is very important for these sports. Ectomorphs need to focus more on heavy weightlifting and minimize (or even ditch) cardio exercises to build muscle mass.

On the nutritional side, ectomorphs also need to eat a lot more than mesomorphs and endomorphs to gain weight. And if the emphasis is on gaining muscle mass, they must eat even more. This is mainly because weightlifting burns more calories than cardio workouts.

One advantage of this somatotype is eating anything without regard for gaining weight easily. Ectomorphs can tolerate high carbohydrate diets with their speedy metabolism, which maximizes physical performance, and is especially useful when lifting weights.

For ectomorphs who are dead serious about gaining weight, their best bet would be foods with very high caloric densities. Supplements and meal replacement products that pack a lot of caloric wallop in significantly smaller servings can be an ectomorph's best friend. These include high-calorie protein shakes and the like.

Mesomorphs

A person with this type of body is one who typically has a medium-built frame and bone structure. They also tend to have considerable levels of lean body mass and, as a result, are more naturally athletic than most people. Typically, mesomorphs gain muscle mass much more easily because of their body's natural ability to produce lots of growth hormones. Because muscles are much more metabolically active than other types of cells in the body, mesomorphs are naturally lean and muscular, unlike ecto and endomorphs.

It's easy for them to bulk up with weight or resistance training, given their genetic predisposition to building muscle. They quickly see results, and as such, have a genetic advantage over endo and ectomorphs.

Along with quick muscle gains comes increased body fat. That's why mesomorphs need to eat the right macronutrient proportions to complement their training.

Nutritionally speaking, mesomorphs can moderately tolerate carbohydrates. This means they may eat relatively more carbohydrates but only within the context of physical training and post-training recovery. Otherwise, they must moderate the number of carbohydrate calories they consume to avoid gaining more body fat than muscle.

Endomorphs

The typical endomorph body is genetically predisposed to having higher body fat levels and tends to have a softer body mass. This is because among the three somatotypes, being an endomorph means having a significantly slower metabolism than ecto and mesomorphs. One of the main reasons for this is they're more insulin dominant – a key factor in quickly gaining body fat and having difficulty losing it.

Fortunately, along with ease of gaining body fat comes a relatively easier time gaining muscle mass. But unlike mesomorphs, endomorphs need to eat and train in specific ways to maximize muscle mass gains and minimize body fat accumulation. That's why being an endomorph with excess weight isn't necessarily a lifelong prison sentence.

Speaking of physical traits, the most common ones associated with being an endomorph include:

- Minimum muscle definition, if any, and a generally soft body
- A naturally round-shaped body
- A propensity to gain body fat easily
- A large bone structure
- Slow metabolism

Despite being more challenged in achieving and maintaining relatively healthy body weight and lean body, endomorphs can still successfully achieve these goals. With the correct nutritional approach and training strategy, fat loss and maintaining a relatively lean body is not an impossible dream.

The Challenge of Losing Weight

As an endomorph, you've probably tried your best to lose excess weight using a variety of diets and exercise programs. And still, you haven't lost those pounds and inches. Why?

Mainly because your genetic disposition is to be insulin dominant instead of being growth hormone dominant. It's essential to understand the role insulin and growth hormones play in your metabolism to understand its repercussions on your weight loss efforts.

Insulin is a hormone produced by your pancreas, and it primarily regulates blood sugar levels. When you eat, your body digests and breaks this food down into glucose - the primary fuel your body uses for daily activities. After successfully doing so, glucose enters your bloodstream to be distributed among your body's cells to provide the necessary nutrients and energy for survival.

Depending on the amount of glucose that enters your bloodstream at any given time, your blood sugar level will rise. If too much glucose enters it too fast, your blood sugar level spikes or increases significantly and quickly. When this happens, your pancreas secretes insulin to bring your blood sugar level down quickly.

At first glance, this seems to have nothing to do with weight loss or weight gain. But when insulin acts on excess blood sugar to normalize its level, it converts it into glycogen for storage in the liver. The organ's capacity for glycogen storage is limited. The glucose overspill is then converted into body fat.

This isn't the only bad news. When blood sugar spikes and crashes become the norm rather than the exception, your pancreas goes under increasing stress to produce more insulin. At one point, your body may develop what is called insulin resistance. Under this condition, the amount of insulin needed to bring blood sugar down to normal levels increases because the body starts to develop *resistance towards it.*

If left uncontrolled, it will eventually result in non-responsiveness to insulin, chronically high blood sugar levels, and eventually diabetes.

More than just significantly impacting your body fat levels, being insulin dominant as an endomorph can also lead to a higher risk of diabetes. That's why part of the endomorph diet's nutritional strategy is to eat the right amount of macronutrients, especially carbohydrates. We'll talk about it in more detail further on.

The other reason why losing weight as an endomorph can be more challenging is the naturally slower metabolism, whether the individual has a sweet tooth or not. Metabolism refers to the rate at which the body can burn calories from the food and drinks consumed daily.

The faster one's metabolism is, the greater his or her daily required calories are. But a slower metabolism means fewer daily required calories. This means that a person with a fast metabolism will not gain weight even after eating a tub of ice cream in one sitting. On the other hand, even just a cone of ice cream can lead to weight gain for a person with a slow metabolism.

Another reason many endomorphs appear to fail in their weight loss goals is because of discouragement or even a simple lack of motivation. Because many of them use inappropriate or ineffective weight loss strategies for their somatotype, they may have gained significant weight over the years. Being heavyset or overweight can make regular exercise more challenging for them. They'll need to use a lot more willpower just to start a diet and a fitness program. Because they experience little to no results compared to the two other somatotypes in the same timeframe, their willpower reserves eventually dry up, and they become demotivated. Thus, they inevitably fail to lose excess weight.

Now, these three challenges appear to make successful weight loss and maintenance impossible for an endomorph. Fortunately, nothing could be further from the truth. It may be more challenging to drop and keep unwanted pounds and inches off as an endomorph. Still, with the proper nutritional and training strategies, you'll be able to accomplish your body weight and fitness goals and keep the fat you lost from creeping back.

Chapter 3: Figuring Out Your "Numbers"

"Cutting back on calories is not the answer to successful weight loss and successful health... you have to increase the quality of what you eat, not just reduce the quantity." - Joel Fuhrman

Although losing weight as an endomorph requires a different diet and training strategy compared to what works for meso and ectomorphs, all three share the same foundational principles governing weight loss. These are the principles of the caloric deficit and macronutrient ratios.

Caloric Deficits

When you look at it, losing weight is not rocket science. The basic formula is fewer calories in and more calories burned equals weight loss. Simply put, all you need to do is eat fewer calories than your body can burn every day, and you burn body fat and weight decreases.

For example, if your body requires at least 2000 calories a day, you need to consume less than that to lose weight. How long should you do it? It will depend on how many pounds you'd like to lose.

How many calories should you burn to lose weight? A pound of body weight is roughly 3,500 calories. So, for example, to lose 20 pounds, you must burn 70,000 calories more than you consume over time.

So, to lose 20 pounds over the next four months, you'll spread the 70,000 calories over roughly 16 weeks at an average of 4375 calories per week. This is the equivalent of roughly 1.25 pounds every seven days. And to accomplish a caloric deficit of 4375 calories every week, you must eat 625 fewer calories than your daily caloric requirements every day.

To lose the same amount of weight but in a shorter period, say in just two months, then you must create a larger daily caloric deficit to achieve this. In this example, wanting to lose the same amount of weight in half the time means doubling your daily and weekly caloric deficits to speed up the process.

It's not that simple, though. There's a tradeoff to losing too much weight too fast. When you try to hurry up your weight loss results, your risk of mainly losing water or muscle mass weight becomes much higher.

You don't want that to happen because, as we've discussed in the previous chapter, what you'd like to accomplish isn't just weight loss per se, but *body fat loss*. When you try to lose too much weight, as is the case with crash diets, you'll end up losing mostly water and muscle mass rather than body fat. If you lose more muscle than body fat, it will affect your metabolism negatively and slow it down, stopping your weight loss progress prematurely.

You may be wondering what the appropriate rate at which to lose weight is to minimize the risk of losing muscle mass along the way. There are many ideas about this, but legitimate weight-loss experts agree that losing between one and two pounds every week is optimal. If you lose less than a pound every week, your weight loss progress will be too slow, and you risk being discouraged and eventually quitting. But if you lose over two pounds every seven days, you maximize your risk of losing significant muscle mass. This will slow down your metabolism, and you'll end up quitting and rebounding, regaining most of the weight you lost, and more.

This is why crash diets aren't just ineffective, but they are also detrimental to your long-term weight-loss efforts and even health. Crash diets are too extreme for most people to realistically sustain them long enough to accomplish their weight loss goals. And even for the select few who may accomplish their weight loss goals by crash dieting, it can take so much out of them emotionally. And usually, the moment they eat regular food, they revert to binge eating because they feel so deprived.

That is why usually those who lose weight with crash diets gain back the pounds they've lost, or worse, they gain more weight. When this happens, they become discouraged and frustrated to where they won't consider dieting again. What's the point of going through so much hell only to regain the weight you lost?

That's why part of the endomorph diet strategy involves "limiting" weight loss to only two pounds a week. Losing excess weight isn't just a one-time event. Remember that you are in this for the long haul; instead of sprinting, think of it as running an ultra-marathon. You need to pace your weight loss progress. This will help you maximize your chances of accomplishing your weight loss goals, maintaining or even improving your health along the way, and keeping the pounds off for good.

Macronutrients

While the basic formula for losing weight is burning more calories than you consume, you must also consider the composition of your total calories. It's because each somatotype is different for burning specific types of calories. And as an endomorph, this is one of the most critical factors that is often neglected.

Macronutrients fall into three general types of calories that can be found in food and drinks. Everything you consume contains one or all these macronutrients: carbohydrates, proteins, and dietary fats. Of course, the exceptions are calorie-free drinks like water, brewed tea, plain black brewed coffee, and foods naturally or modified to have no calories.

Many healthy and sensible weight-loss diets prescribe getting as much as 55%, 30%, and 15% of once-daily caloric requirements from carbohydrates, proteins, and fats, respectively. And for many people, it works for as long as the proper caloric deficits are regularly achieved. But for endomorphs, these ratios are not appropriate. Why?

Remember that one of the key characteristics of endomorphs is being insulin dominant. You're genetically predisposed to be less efficient than ectomorphs and mesomorphs in metabolizing carbohydrate calories. Considering this, getting more than half of your daily caloric requirements from carbohydrates may stop you from losing weight despite constantly maintaining caloric deficits.

As an endomorph, your ideal macronutrient ratios should be 25% carbohydrates, 35% proteins, and 40% healthy dietary fats. If your daily caloric requirement is 2000 calories, its breakdown would be:

- 500 calories from carbohydrates
- 700 calories from proteins
- 800 calories from healthy dietary fats

You should apply the macronutrient ratios to your total daily caloric required deficit. To minimize losing mostly muscle and maximize losing body fat, strive to lose a maximum of 2 pounds only every week. Given there are about 3500 calories per pound, your maximum weekly caloric deficit must not exceed 7000 calories. Spreading it over seven days, you should reduce your daily caloric intake by no more than 1000 calories. In other words, your daily caloric deficit should be no more than 1000 calories.

Going back to our example, if your daily caloric requirement is 2000 calories, your daily caloric deficit should not exceed 1000 calories. This means you should consume at least 1000 calories a day to avoid overdoing it. If your daily requirement is 3000 calories, you must consume at least 2000 calories daily.

Notice that despite being insulin dominant as an endomorph, a ketogenic diet isn't recommended. Carbohydrates are still allowed but only to a maximum of 25% of your daily caloric consumption. Why is that?

Most people fail to sustain extreme diets like the ketogenic diet because they are too hard to implement in the long run. In a ketogenic diet, people are forced to go for extremely long periods without carbohydrates, which is the body's primary fuel source and one of the most emotionally satisfying types of food around. Trying to go without something that makes life so much more satisfying and is the body's primary fuel source can be emotionally and intellectually taxing. That's why in the long run, many people who go through extreme diets fail to sustain them and, worse, gain back all the weight they lost – and even more.

More than just the risk of failed weight loss, extreme diets can also affect your health eventually. For example, overdoing the keto diet can lead to a condition known as ketogenic acidosis. This means your blood becomes highly acidic, leading to more complex health issues like long-term kidney failure and hypertension. Limiting or even eliminating one macronutrient for another is a recipe for health deterioration over the long term. It's good to remember that no single macronutrient type can lead to success or result in utter failure. There's a reason God or the universe created these three macronutrients, and that's because our bodies need them. When we gain weight or become sick because we overeat, we shouldn't blame macronutrients. We must point the finger at ourselves instead.

That's why the endomorph diet does not promote nutritional extremism but sensible, moderate, and healthy weight loss. Ultimately, the main benefit of losing excess weight is improved health. Looking good is just a bonus.

How Many Calories Do You Need Every Day?

You may be wondering how many calories you need to maintain your weight. This is crucial because this magic number is key to determining your daily caloric deficit and specific numbers of macronutrients. Fortunately, figuring this out isn't rocket science.

Your Basal Metabolic Rate (BMR)

BMR pertains to the approximate number of calories your body needs to maintain its weight and function normally in a state of rest. In other words, it tells you the minimum calories you need every day to maintain your body weight if you do nothing throughout the day.

One of the most popular and accurate ways to determine your basal metabolic rate is through the Harris-Benedict Equation. Here are the formulas to find your basal metabolic rate:

For Men: BMR = 10 x weight (kg) + 6.25 x height (cm) – 5 x age (years) + 5

For Women: BMR = 10 x weight (kg) + 6.25 x height (cm) – 5 x age (years) – 161

Please take note that you must convert your weight in pounds to kilograms and your height in feet or inches to centimeters to calculate your BMR properly. To convert your weight (pounds) and height (inches) to metric units, multiply your weight by 2.43 and your height by 2.54.

Let's say you're a guy who stands 178 centimeters (roughly 6 feet tall), weighs 91 kilos (a little over 200 pounds), and is 40 years old. Applying the Harris-Benedict formula, your estimated BMR is:

BMR = 10 x 91kg + 6.25 x 178 cm – (5 x 40 years old) + 5

BMR = 910 + 437.50 – 200 + 5

BMR = 1,827.50 calories

Your basal metabolic rate doesn't consider your daily physical activity levels. To estimate your total daily energy expenditure (TDEE), multiply your BMR by a specific number corresponding to your daily physical activity level. The physical activity levels are:

- Sedentary, with minimal to no exercise = 1.2

- Lightly active or engages in light exercise/sports up to three times weekly = 1.375

- Moderately active or exercises up to five times weekly = 1.55

- Very active or engaging in strenuous exercise six to seven days a week = 1.725

- Extra active or performs very hard exercises or engages in a job that's physically demanding = 1.90

Going back to our example, if you're a 40-year-old man at 178 centimeters tall, weighing 91 kilos, your estimated TDEE based on your current physical activity level is:

- 2193 calories daily if you are living a sedentary lifestyle

- 2512.81 calories if you're lightly active

- 2832.63 calories if you're moderately active

- 3152.44 calories if you are very active

- 3472.25 calories if you are extra active

If you're a woman, your formula for BMR will be slightly different. Instead of adding five to the end of the formula, you will subtract 161. Doing so takes into consideration the physiological differences in metabolism between men and women. Using the formula and assuming you stand 150 centimeters tall, weigh 60 kilograms, and are 40 years of age, your estimated basal metabolic rate would be:

BMR = 10 x 60kg + 6.25 x 150 cm − (5 x 40 years old) -161

BMR = 600 + 937.50 - 200.00 − 161

BMR = 1,176.50 calories

Considering your daily physical activity level, the following are the numbers by which you must multiply your BMR and their corresponding TDEE levels:

- Sedentary, with minimal to no exercise = 1.2 X 1,176.50 calories = 1,411.80

- Lightly active or engages in light exercise/sports up to 3 times weekly = 1.375 X 1,176.50 calories = 1,617.69

- Moderately active or exercises up to 5 times weekly = 1.55 X 1,176.50 calories = 1,823.58

- Very active or engaging in strenuous exercise 6 to 7 days a week = 1.725 X 1,176.50 calories = 2,029.46

- Extra active or performs very hard exercises or engages in a physically demanding job = 1.90 X 1,176.50 calories = 2,235.35

In both examples, being physically active gives you the benefit of eating more by way of higher total daily energy expenditure numbers. If only for this, you should be encouraged to exercise regularly. But having more caloric leeway isn't the main reason you should do so.

Now, I get that not everyone is a numbers person. If you want a magic black box that will automatically calculate your BMR and TDEE, you can go to *https://www.omnicalculator.com/health/bmr-harris-benedict-equation* and simply plug in your numbers. Don't forget to click on the Advanced Mode button to include your physical activity level to compute your TDEE.

Cutting Calories the Right Way

Losing weight is conceptually simple: consume fewer calories than your body needs regularly. Now that you know how many calories you require every day, the next step is determining the number of calories you must cut to accomplish your goals.

One of the biggest mistakes people make when dieting is assuming that they can cut as many calories as possible to lose as much weight as they want - as quickly as possible. But it's not that simple. There is a point at which cutting too many calories regularly can lead to weight loss stagnation and long-term damage to the metabolism.

Why's that? The human body was designed to be a very intelligent machine. To a certain extent, it's like a financial manager that is very good at budgeting. The only difference is that instead of money or other financial resources, it budgets its regular calorie allocations.

Your body has a built-in survival mechanism that operates 24/7, even if you're not aware of it. Besides oxygen and water, calories are crucial to your survival. Your body instinctively knows this and makes sure it has enough calories to survive as long as possible.

When you go on crash diets or other diets that use extreme caloric restrictions, you may lose a lot of weight in the first several days. One pitfall of rapid weight loss is the possibility of mainly losing muscle mass and retained water rather than body fat. The other pitfall is short-lived weight loss.

As a natural caloric budget manager, your body will finally catch on to the fact that it's getting fewer calories than it is used to. Just like any responsible financial manager, it will adjust its caloric spending to stretch its caloric budget and ensure survival for long.

While you know this isn't a permanent situation, and you won't die from starvation, your body doesn't. As a survival response, it will slow down the rate at which it burns or metabolizes calories. When this happens, you'll start to burn fewer calories daily, overcoming the caloric deficits that are meant to help you lose excess weight. We call this a *weight loss plateau*. It's even possible for you to gain extra weight, depending on the extent of your metabolic slowdown.

Now that you know that you shouldn't drastically cut calories to lose weight and keep it off successfully, what's the limit in creating regular caloric deficits? While there are no fixed or industry benchmarks, a 10% to 15% daily caloric deficit appears to be the consensus among many health and fitness experts. So, if your computed total daily energy expenditure is 2000 calories, reduce your daily caloric intake by 200 to 300 calories. This means your total daily caloric intake should be between 1700 and 1800 calories.

You'll need to focus more on medium to long-term weight loss instead of shredding body fat rapidly. By limiting your daily caloric deficits to between 10% and 15%, you'll be able to successfully lose body fat with minimal risks of metabolic slowdown and quitting abruptly. You'll be running a marathon instead of a sprint, i.e., you go much further and achieve long-lasting weight loss.

Focus on Weekly Totals

Life can undoubtedly throw curveballs at you now and then. There may also be times when you must cut your caloric deficit for important things in life, like family celebration dinners or quality time with your spouse. When these happen, it's okay. The important thing is to achieve your weekly total caloric deficit.

Focusing on weekly totals also gives you more elbow room while dieting. It's also much less stressful knowing you can compensate on days you cannot achieve your required caloric deficits.

So how can you achieve this? Let's say your target weekly caloric deficit is 3500 calories, which equals about one pound of body fat. Spreading it out across seven days means an average daily caloric deficit of 500 calories.

Let's say your caloric deficit for today fell short by 100 calories. You can make up for it by adding it to one of the remaining days of the week, bumping up the daily deficit to 600 calories.

Taking Caloric Deficit Breaks

Earlier, we talked about how your body is smart enough to sense extended periods of the caloric deficit and make the necessary adjustments to your metabolism. While limiting your daily caloric deficits between 10% and 15% is optimum for gradual weight loss, doing it for too long may trigger your body to start saving calories.

To avoid this, bump up your caloric intake by up to 10% every 4th or 5th day of your diet. By doing this, you'll be able to convince your body that there is no famine. As a result, it won't slow down your metabolism and will continue as usual. This is one key to sustainable and healthy weight loss.

Endomorph Ideal Macros

As mentioned earlier, simply determining your total required number of calories isn't enough. This is especially true if you are an endomorph. That's why, besides determining your total daily caloric intake net of the ideal deficit, you must also determine the number of calories you need from each specific macronutrient every day.

Earlier, we talked about the ideal macronutrient ratio for losing weight, also known as cutting in fitness circles. The consensus is 25%, 35%, and 40% of your total daily calories should come from carbohydrates, proteins, and healthy dietary fats, respectively. By implementing this macronutrient ratio strategy regularly, you can optimize your chances of successfully losing excess weight, mostly body fat.

While this book's emphasis is on weight loss, you can also use the general principles to achieve two other weight-related goals: maintenance and gaining weight. After all, diets are nutritional strategies meant to accomplish several weight-related goals, such as losing weight or achieving normal blood chemistry levels. So, you can use the endomorph diet to ensure you maintain your ideal body weight and lean body mass. And to look more muscular, you can also use it to increase your lean muscle mass.

You'll need to tweak it a bit in terms of macronutrient ratios to shift to weight maintenance or weight gain mode. Let's talk about your three possible goals on the endomorph diet and how it pertains to macronutrient ratios.

Weight Loss or Cutting Phase

For most endomorphs, the primary weight-related goal is fat loss. As you have learned, this somatotype tends to accumulate body fat at a much faster rate compared to ectomorphs and endomorphs. Also, endomorphs have a much harder time losing excess body fat or cutting weight than the two.

Part of what causes these two challenges is relative difficulty metabolizing carbohydrate calories. And one of the most significant factors contributing to this limitation is the tendency for endomorphs to be more insulin dominant rather than growth hormone dominant. Insulin dominance leads to lower insulin sensitivity, a significant contributor to unwanted weight gains and failed attempts to lose excess body fat among endomorphs.

Because of these, the primary nutritional strategy for shedding excess body fat is to significantly reduce carbohydrate consumption and, instead, increase the consumption of healthy dietary fats. Why?

While protein is mainly used to maintain and build muscle mass, consuming too much of it may also result in excess insulin production. This does not bode well for endomorphs because they are more insulin dominant rather than growth hormone dominant.

But healthy dietary fat offers several benefits to successfully shedding excess weight. For one, dietary fat is more satiating than carbohydrates; you will likely feel fuller for longer, minimizing your risk of overeating at every meal.

Another key weight loss-related benefit of increasing healthy dietary fat consumption is caloric density. Compared to carbohydrates and protein, dietary fats pack more calories per gram of volume. Every gram of carbohydrate and protein contains approximately four calories, while dietary fats contain around nine calories per gram. This means you don't have to eat a lot of food to accomplish your daily caloric goals. And considering its higher satiation levels, eating less shouldn't be that big of a problem with healthy fats.

Take note that the term *healthy* is used with *dietary fats*. It's because not all fats are created equal. Eating the wrong fats will not just present setbacks with your weight loss efforts but also significantly impact your overall health.

What are healthy dietary fats? These are monounsaturated and polyunsaturated fats. More than just helping you achieve your body fat shedding goals as an endomorph, these also help minimize significant health risks. Some of the best healthy dietary fat sources include olive oil, virgin coconut oil, and fatty fish like salmon.

It's worth noting that you will only have to significantly reduce carbohydrate intake on the endomorph diet and not eliminate or severely restrict it. There are two excellent reasons for this.

First, carbohydrates are the primary fuel source for the body. It's because it's more easily accessible and provides fast-acting energy. And going on extremely low or no carbohydrate diets risks a condition known as ketoacidosis. Your blood can become highly acidic when you overdo carbohydrate cutting.

Another critical reason to avoid severe carbohydrate restrictions or eliminating them is to avoid overtaxing your willpower reserves, burning out, and quitting altogether. Let's face it, carbohydrate-rich foods help make life more pleasurable. With all the stresses from other areas of your life, severely depriving yourself of carbohydrate-related joys can lead to a higher level of chronic stress. This maximizes your risks of quitting early and not accomplishing your weight loss goals.

Just like dietary fats, there are good and not so good carbohydrate calories. What distinguishes one from the other is the glycemic index. Also called GI, it measures the speed at which your body can break down specific types of carbohydrate foods into their readily usable form, which is glucose. The higher the glycemic index is, the faster it's converted into glucose and enters your bloodstream. The lower a carbohydrate-rich food's glycemic index is, the opposite is true. Your body breaks it down into glucose at a much slower pace, which leads to a more stable and steadier entry into the bloodstream.

For most of your carbohydrate calories, you must focus on low GI sources, so your body converts them to glucose at a slower rate, entering the bloodstream at a much steadier pace instead of being dumped all at once. This helps you achieve stable blood sugar levels, minimizing or avoiding blood sugar spikes and crashes.

When your blood sugar levels are steady, you feel alert and energetic throughout most of the day. When your blood sugar levels are volatile, which happens when most of your carbohydrate intake comprises high GI variants, you will most likely fluctuate between feeling high and energetic one minute, then sluggish and sleepy the next.

Frequent blood sugar spikes and crashes can severely affect your productivity during the day. It will be challenging to do things when you frequently feel sluggish and sleepy after work. It can even lead to higher chronic stress that can significantly affect your ability to stick to the endomorph diet and exercise plan.

When you're chronically under a lot of stress, the tendency to break the diet becomes much higher. Particularly if you're an emotional eater, failure to manage stress well can severely compromise your efforts to shed excess body fat.

What are examples of good carbohydrates, i.e., low GI ones? They include whole-grain foods, brown rice, and oats. We'll look at the best foods to eat in the endomorph diet, including carbohydrates, in the next chapter.

Maintenance Phase

After losing excess weight and achieving your desired body weight, it's time to move onto the next stage, maintenance mode. After all, what good is it to lose excess weight only to gain it back soon after? All the work and effort you put into accomplishing your weight loss goals will just be for nothing.

One challenge of being an endomorph is maintaining the ideal weight, particularly maintenance calories. Going off track and overeating may lead to significant re-accumulation of body fat, even for just a couple of days. Again, the reasons for this are that endomorphs have relatively slower metabolisms and tend to be insulin dominant. That's why the bigger chunk of losing weight is the maintenance phase. And it's not about lack of discipline and determination, though these are critical components. An equally big reason for this is beyond your control because it is normal human physiology.

When you enter the maintenance phase of the endomorph diet, the first thing you must do is bump up your daily calorie intake. However, there is a limit to how much you can do that, and that ceiling is your estimated total daily energy requirements or TDEE.

Remember, you consume fewer calories during the fat loss phase than your body needs to function normally and maintain its current mass. To maintain your desired body weight, you must consume approximately the same number of calories as your TDEE to avoid losing any more weight.

At this point, your macronutrient ratios stay the same because of the tendency to be insulin dominant and, as a result, have a more difficult time burning carbohydrate calories. Hence, 25%, 35%, and 40% of your total daily calories should come from carbohydrates, protein, and healthy dietary fats, respectively.

Bulking Phase

Here, we're not talking about simply gaining weight for the sake of doing so. Suppose the desired weight loss involves mainly losing body fat, bulking up, or gaining weight. In that case, it focuses on gaining *lean muscle mass.* Why would you consider doing this after you've already accomplished your desired body weight?

One of the main benefits of having more muscle mass is a faster metabolism. Among all types of cells in the body, muscles burn the most calories. Thus, increasing your muscle mass can make it easier for you to stay in shape, even if you don't strictly watch what you eat.

I'm not saying that gaining more muscle mass gives you the license to be lax in your diet and ditch calorie counting and macronutrient ratios. On days you cannot stay within your limits, you minimize your chances of accumulating excess body fat. Even if you gain fat, it won't be as much compared to having less muscle mass.

I'd like to clarify that regarding "bulking up" or increasing muscle mass, you're highly unlikely to look like a professional bodybuilder despite your best efforts to do so. Especially if you're a woman, adding muscle to your frame won't make you look like a man even if you tried.

Contrary to what many people believe, becoming muscularly huge is only possible for a select few. For one, you need to have the right genetics to achieve the physique of professional bodybuilders. It's estimated that only 1% to 2% of the world's entire population is genetically gifted to become professional bodybuilders. If only because of this, your chances of looking like an overly muscular ninja turtle are practically nil.

Let's say that, for the sake of argument, you belong to that 1% to 2%. It's still not a guarantee that you'll be able to grow your muscles to out of this world proportions. It takes a special kind of training regimen to do that. Part of that involves training very heavily and lifting outrageous weights to grow your muscles. Developing enough strength and power to do so takes a long time, and this is not something you can do in just a few weeks or months. Hence, your risks of looking like Arnold Schwarzenegger in his prime or Dwayne the Rock Johnson are very low regardless of how hard you work out at the gym.

Also, those mass monster bodybuilders you see in magazines and on YouTube didn't get that massive simply because of genetics and hard work. They had to eat a lot of food. If you think that's fun, think about how you feel after eating at an open buffet. Now, imagine doing that almost every day or in a single sitting for every meal. You'll probably feel nauseated when you learn about how much food, especially chicken breasts, professional bodybuilders need to eat daily.

Finally, all the hard work, discipline and voluminous eating, and genetics in the world will mean nothing if you don't take steroids and other muscle-building drugs. Bodybuilders can achieve enough muscle mass to compete at the highest levels of competition because of performance and physique-enhancing drugs. These are not only expensive, but they're dangerous to your health. Many famous bodybuilders have died at a relatively young age due to the complications of steroid use and the abuse of other physique-enhancing drugs.

Now that you see how hard it is to achieve the physique of a mass monster bodybuilder, you should feel at ease about adding lean muscle mass to your physique.

As an endomorph, weight loss and weight maintenance are the most challenging phases because of the propensity to gain body fat quickly. Gaining weight should be the easiest phase of the three.

By adding more muscles to your frame, you'll inadvertently gain body fat too. Fortunately, you can minimize this while maximizing muscle mass gain with the right exercises and caloric consumption.

Because your goal is to add muscle mass and, consequently, weight, you'll be striving for daily caloric surpluses instead of deficits. And just like when you were trying to lose excess weight, also decide on a cap in terms of your daily surplus. Otherwise, you increase your risk of gaining more body fat than muscle mass. Ideally, your daily caloric surplus should not exceed 10% of your TDEE. By doing it this way, you give your body enough time to acclimatize to the changes and minimize the risk of gaining excess body fat.

For example, add up to 200 calories at most to your daily consumption if your computed TDEE is 2000 calories. As for macronutrient ratios, stick to the standard ratios of 25%, 35%, and 40% for carbs, protein, and healthy dietary fat, respectively. Give it a week or two. If you gain weight and your body fat percentage increases instead of your lean body mass, or the increase is greater than the rate of muscle gain, you must adjust your macronutrient ratios. You may particularly need to adjust your macronutrient ratios. Here's what it can look like ~ 35% carbohydrates, 30% dietary fat, and 35% protein.

You may be wondering why the percentage of carbohydrate calories increased while dietary fats were reduced, and protein was kept steady. By increasing total calories, your daily protein calories will automatically increase even if its ratio stays the same. This ensures you still get enough protein to feed your muscle growth.

The increased carbohydrate intake is vital so you can work out harder at the gym, i.e., lift heavier weights and do more reps and sets for greater stimulation of muscle growth. Muscles only grow through resistance or strength training. Also, doing so means a greater afterburn effect, which refers to your body's tendency to keep its metabolism elevated long after you have worked out.

So, to lift more and perform more reps and sets, you'll need more carbs to be able to do so. Hence, the increase in carbohydrate calorie percentage.

Chapter 4: What to Eat and What to Avoid

Considering that endomorphs are insulin dominant and have a much harder time processing carbohydrate calories, the most essential dietary change involves cutting back on carbohydrate calories. Take note that the operative term here is "cutting back" and not "eliminating" or "severely restricting," as in the case with extreme diets like the keto diet.

Carbohydrates are not inherently evil, contrary to what many pseudo-experts proclaim! God didn't make carbohydrates to be detested but to be the human body's most efficient fuel source. The only distinction for endomorphs is that it's harder to process carbohydrate calories. But just like ectomorphs and mesomorphs, endomorphs still need carbs, albeit in smaller amounts.

Severely restricting carbohydrate calories or, worse, eliminating them for extended periods can be detrimental to your health. It can cause your blood to become acidic, the technical term for which is ketoacidosis.

By simply cutting back on carbs and limiting or avoiding high-glycemic-index ones, you can lose weight and, more importantly, *keep it off.* There is no need for extreme measures that can jeopardize your long-term weight management and health.

Consuming mostly low or medium GI carbs helps address another key factor that hinders fat loss: insulin dominance resulting from poor insulin sensitivity. Because low/mid GI carbs don't trigger as much insulin production as high GI ones, your insulin sensitivity can improve over time. This helps address your insulin dominance issue en route to successfully losing weight.

To help you minimize consumption of high GI carbs, or avoid them altogether, remember that foods with a glycemic index of 70 and above are considered high GI. The lower the GI, the better.

According to Harvard University, here's a list of the best carbohydrate foods for endomorphs. These are low to mid-GI items and, more important, contain high amounts of dietary fiber that are important for improving insulin sensitivity.

- Kidney Beans (GI of 24)
- Lentils (GI of 32)
- Raw Apples (GI of 36)
- Boiled Carrots (GI of 39)
- Quinoa (GI of 51)
- Steel-Cut or Rolled Oats (55)
- Sweet Potatoes (GI of 63)
- Couscous (GI of 65)
- Brown Rice (GI of 68)

Minimize consumption of carbohydrates that aren't on this list. Save them for special occasions or cheat days, instead. These include soda, fruit juices, energy drinks, candies, cakes, and donuts.

Suppose you can't avoid eating high-GI carbohydrates (70 and above). There, you can reduce their GI by eating them with proteins or dietary fats, which have very low GIs or none at all. GI measurements hold true only when foods are eaten alone. But with mixing, combining relatively higher-GI foods with low or no GI can help make them more insulin friendly, i.e., lower their GIs.

For example, the GI of white rice eaten with lean chicken breast becomes lower because of the chicken's low GI nature. Hence, always eat a complete meal that contains more protein and fat calories than carbohydrates.

Protein Sources

The best protein sources are chicken and turkey breasts, eggs, and lean cuts of beef and pork. These pack the most proteins per serving and contain dietary fats, too, which can help you achieve your daily target macros easier.

Chicken breasts are particularly popular, especially among bodybuilders. They pack a lot of lean protein, which is crucial to maintain muscle mass while dieting for shows.

Dietary Fats

Given that dietary fat calories are the biggest macros for the endomorph diet, it can be pretty challenging to get them all from the fat content of your protein sources, i.e., meat and seafood. Hence, it's essential to supplement with excellent sources like virgin coconut oil and medium-chain triglyceride (MCT) oils. They're two of the healthiest and most practical sources of healthy fat calories to ensure you get enough calories from this macronutrient. Best of all, they don't trigger insulin production in your body!

Pantry Stocks

The best way to stick to the endomorph diet is to make sure your pantry's stocked with the right kinds of food, so your risks of having to order processed food from outside sources are minimized. If you have the right foods in your pantry, you'll have greater control over your diet. Here are a few of the most important items you should stock at home.

Carbohydrates

- Oatmeal
- Brown Rice
- Quinoa
- Legumes
- Sweet Potatoes

Protein

- Chicken Breast
- Organic or Free-Range Eggs
- Leaner Cuts of Beef and Pork (Tenderloin, etc.)
- Canned Tuna
- Lentils
- Salmon

Fats

- Grass-Fed Butter
- Virgin Coconut Oil
- MCT Oil
- Olive Oil
- Flaxseed Oil
- Peanuts
- Almonds

- Walnuts

Fruits and Vegetables

- Lettuce
- Cabbage
- Cucumber
- Celery
- Spinach
- Tomatoes
- Onions
- Garlic
- Apples
- Grapefruit
- Berries

Others

- Stevia
- Erythritol Sweetener
- Salt and Pepper

Chapter 5: Intermittent Fasting for Endomorphs

Have you heard these?

> Don't skip meals.

> Always eat breakfast because it's the most important meal of the day.

> Always have something to eat just in case you go hungry.

I'd guess that your answer is a resounding "yes!" You may have heard these from your parents (especially your mother), your aunts and uncles, your teachers, or your spouse. They certainly mean well, and they are simply concerned with your health and well-being, but expressions of care like these are misinformed. In particular, going hungry for extended periods isn't necessarily harmful to you.

Over the last decade, studies show hunger isn't as bad as people think. Intentionally going hungry can be beneficial to our health if done right.

Also, intentionally going hungry isn't something new. People across the globe and from different cultures have been doing it since time immemorial. It's called fasting. Fasting regularly is called intermittent fasting.

Fasting has been around far longer than most people think. It's an integral part of many of the world's religions, and many people fast for spiritual reasons.

But in the last decade or two, more people are getting into the practice for health and fitness reasons. Many testify that fasting regularly provides significant benefits. With more people openly sharing the gospel of fasting as a lifestyle, an increasing number of curious people have adopted the practice.

Intermittent fasting simply means fasting regularly. And by regularly, intermittent fasting differs from religious or spiritual fasting.

Fasting for religious purposes is often done within the context of the general membership in organized religions. Often, regular fasting means annual fasting as a religious practice. Of all the world's major religions today, Islam has the most grueling type of regular fasting. While done once a year only during the holy month of Ramadan, its followers fast daily for one whole month.

In Christianity, fasting isn't as extensive. During the Lent season, Catholics are only required to abstain from eating meat on Fridays. Fasting by skipping meals is mostly optional, and Catholics and Evangelicals usually do it as a spiritual discipline meant to sharpen their spiritual senses.

Regular, in the context of intermittent fasting, means every day or several days during the week. In other words, intermittent fasting is a lifestyle instead of an occasional practice. You can fast intermittently in different ways or by using different protocols. What differentiates one protocol from another are the duration, frequency, and the food and drinks allowed.

For example, one fasting protocol may require fasting for 16 hours every day while another only requires a day or two every week but for over 24 hours. One fasting protocol permits eating certain types of food during the fasting hours, while another only allows water and other calorie-free beverages during the same period.

How Intermittent Fasting Works

One of the things that makes people unique is how their bodies respond to food. For example, some people are allergic to shrimp while others have no problem indulging in them. Another example is diabetics, whose condition prevents them from properly metabolizing sugars. If they ate normally (in terms of simple carbohydrates or sugary foods like non-diabetics do), they might suffer from significant health complications like failed kidneys and gangrene.

In the same way, your body reacts differently to different states. By this, I mean states of hunger and being fed. Some people take several hours to completely digest the food and drinks they consume to convert them into readily usable energy for their mental and physical activities. In your case, the process may be significantly shorter, depending on your physiology and genetics.

If your body gets enough calories through food and drinks, it's safe to say that you can do what you need to do throughout the day. It's because there is enough energy by way of calories to power it throughout the day. It's also possible to consume more calories than are needed and end up gaining body fat. This is why overeating, i.e., consuming more calories than your body requires, can lead to a chronic caloric surplus and, ultimately, excess body fat or weight. Essentially, body fat is nothing more than excess calories stored in your body.

Intermittent fasting can help you lose body fat and, ultimately, excess body weight in a couple of ways. First, it helps you to achieve caloric deficits even if you do not count calories. By fasting for several hours during the day or night, you're naturally able to reduce the number of calories consumed daily.

Now you may be wondering ˜if the endomorph diet already requires daily caloric deficits, why even considering combining it with intermittent fasting? The main reason is because of one key benefit associated with it: improved hormone levels.

First, intermittent fasting (or *IF*) can help your body increase its production of fat-burning hormones. Fasting intermittently can help you burn more body fat than simply cutting down on calories. Particularly, IF can help increase the production of human growth hormones and norepinephrine. These are beneficial hormones in terms of burning off excess fat.

Another way intermittent fasting can significantly complement the endomorph diet is by regulating your appetite. It does so by increasing and decreasing two critical hormones associated with appetite: leptin and ghrelin. IF can help your body increase leptin, which is the hormone responsible for feeling satiated. It can also help your body reduce ghrelin levels, i.e., the hunger hormone. Done correctly, you'll feel less hungry and satiated for more extended periods. These can help make weight loss and maintenance much easier for you as an endomorph.

And finally, intermittent fasting can help improve your body's insulin sensitivity. Remember that as an endomorph, the tendency to be insulin dominant is one of the critical factors that make it more challenging to lose weight. This can make your body less sensitive to insulin over the long term, which puts you at higher risk not just for gaining weight but also for diabetes.

By helping improve your insulin sensitivity, your body will process carbohydrates much better and minimize the tendency to store them as body fat. Optimal insulin sensitivity also makes it easier for your body to break down stored body fat for energy, making it much easier to lose unwanted pounds.

However, fasting intermittently is an excellent supplement to the endomorph diet. How do you do it? There are many ways but let's talk about four of the most popular ways of doing it, i.e., intermittent fasting protocols.

LeanGains

This is probably the most popular intermittent fasting protocol, also called the 16/8 diet. This IF protocol's primary objective is maximizing the ratio of lean body mass, total mass, i.e., body composition. Compared to the other protocols, its emphasis on improving the ratio of lean body mass, total mass makes weight loss a secondary goal and body fat loss the primary one.

It is possible to look thinner and leaner even if you do not lose weight or gain a couple of pounds, as long as you have lost significant body fat. You can gain a little muscle mass, but you will look tighter and fitter if you lose body fat.

LeanGains is called the 16/8 diet because you will fast for 16 hours every day with a feeding window of eight hours. Incorporating LeanGains into the endomorph diet means you have eight hours every day to eat and consume your daily caloric targets.

For women, their physiological makeup requires a slight adjustment in the fasting and feeding hours is needed. Instead of a 16/8 fasting-feeding protocol, it'll be 14/10 or 14 hours of fasting followed by a 10-hour feeding window.

During the fasting hours, LeanGains is a relatively stricter protocol compared to the others. You're not allowed to drink or eat anything that has calories. This protocol only allows calorie-free drinks such as water, unsweetened black coffee, and unsweetened brewed tea. Depending on who you ask, you may also consider sugar-free or diet soda.

But for scheduling your fasting and feeding hours, you have complete freedom over them. The best time to schedule your fasting hours is from the early evening until around lunchtime. Why?

By doing this, you schedule the bulk of your fasting hours while you're asleep. That means you only need to resist the allure of food for half the duration of your fasting hours, assuming you get eight hours of sleep every night. This can help make intermittent fasting easier because you don't have to expend a lot of willpower when skipping meals.

Also, you're already fasting intermittently because you don't eat while you're asleep at night. By scheduling it to start in the early evening, you only have to concern yourself with getting used to fasting for eight waking hours.

The best part of the 16/8 or 14/10 diet is you can schedule your feeding window during the most important times, which is when you're awake – when you need more calories, and you can savor the foods you eat and the beverages you drink while awake. And more importantly, you can spread your total daily calories across the entire eight hours.

One reason for the immense popularity of this IF protocol is simplicity. In its original form, there's no need to count calories or be concerned with the kinds of foods to eat. As a standalone diet, all you need to concern yourself with is when to eat and when not to.

But since you're going to incorporate this as part of your endomorph diet, it won't be as simple. You need to make sure you eat the correct number of calories, including adhering to the proper macronutrient ratios, during the feeding windows.

Another benefit of this protocol you can enjoy while doing the endomorph diet is *time flexibility.* While the best time to schedule your daily fasts is from early evening until around lunchtime the next day, it's not a hard and fast rule. If there are days you need to eat earlier in the morning or aren't able to eat at noontime, you can easily move the windows accordingly. So, if you need to eat later than usual regardless of the reason, don't worry about the diet.

As much as the LeanGains protocol is an efficient and simple one, it has its share of challenges. One of them: this is a legitimate fast. In other words, you really can eat nothing during your food restriction hours. This can be quite an adjustment, especially if you're used to eating smaller and more frequent meals throughout the day. Fortunately, you can get used to it over time.

Also, you can apply a simple workaround to this challenge as a beginner. You don't have to fast for the entire prescribed number of hours but instead, take baby steps. For example, you can start by eating your last meal of the day 30 minutes earlier during the first week. If you usually have dinner or eat your last meal by 8:00 pm, move it to 7:30 for the first few days.

When you get used to it, move it back by another 30 minutes, or in this example, to 7:00 pm or until you can eat your last meal when you want to start your intermittent fasting. When you achieve that, you can delay your breakfast by 30 minutes to one hour and gradually increase the delay until completing the daily 16-or 14-hour fasts comfortably.

Chances are, fasting is something alien to you, as is the case with most people. By gradually easing into the fasting protocol, you can minimize your risks of quitting and optimize your chances of successfully adopting this as part of your endomorph diet lifestyle.

And without trying to sound like a broken record, scheduling your fasting hours starting early evening (between 6 to 8 pm) gives you a head start since you're already fasting while sleeping at night. If you schedule your fasting hours mostly during your waking hours, the mental and physical stresses can be significantly higher, increasing the chances you burn out and quit.

Another common challenge with this protocol is the need to schedule your exercise sessions to coincide or fall within your feeding windows. This is because your body needs calories the most before and after working out. Pre-workout meals ensure you have enough energy to perform exercises correctly and sufficiently. In contrast, post-workout meals help your body recover faster, especially your muscles.

Working out on an empty stomach can prevent you from exercising optimally and increases the risk of injuries when you continue exercising in a weakened state.

Eat-Stop-Eat

Eat-Stop-Eat is the preferred intermittent fasting protocol for people already eating clean and healthy because, unlike LeanGains, Eat-Stop-Eat is all about moderation.

You can eat anything you want but in moderate amounts, whether it's donuts, pizza, or hamburgers. For as long as you eat in moderate amounts, nothing is literally off the table during your feeding hours.

If your diet is already clean and healthy, to begin with, chances are most of the food and drinks you want to consume are already conducive for weight loss. But still, moderate amounts are needed because too much of anything can be harmful.

So, how does Eat-Stop-Eat work? Of all the popular if protocols, this is the simplest and easiest to implement. It's because you don't have to fast every day, but instead, you only need to fast for two non-consecutive days every week. For the remaining five days, you can eat normally. And within the context of the endomorph diet, it means eating the right kinds of foods and getting the correct number of total and macro calories.

You'll need to fast for the entire 24 hours of each of those two fasting days. Put another way; you must go without food or drinks with calories for 24 hours – *twice a week.*

Part of the challenge with this protocol is the length of each fasting period. The tradeoff for fasting less frequently is duration. You don't have to go hungry every day, but you must fast much longer for two out of seven days, i.e., 24 hours.

Another challenge with this protocol is the need for absolute caloric deficit - or 0 calories - twice a week. For most people, not eating for 24 hours can be very challenging to pull off. This is particularly true for people who have never fasted in their lives. It's like trying to go from zero to 100 mph in just five seconds!

Also, zero calories twice a week can lead to over-dieting and may cause substantial muscle mass loss over time; not good because what you want to accomplish is fat loss more than simply losing weight.

Fortunately, there are also workarounds to these challenges. On the challenge of long fasting periods, you can always start by taking small steps. On the days that you fast, start by skipping breakfast first. If breakfast is an indispensable meal for you, start by skipping any other meal for the first few times. Once you become comfortable skipping that specific meal twice a week, up the ante by skipping another one. Once you're comfortable with skipping two out of three or for meals twice a week on non-consecutive days, skip another one until you can fast for 24 hours.

Always remember, there should be at least one day between your two fasting days within the week. Fasting for 48 hours is neither healthy nor effective for long-term weight loss. It can also significantly affect the way you perform at work or school.

Another way to minimize the stress and challenge of fasting for 24 hours twice a week is by scheduling them on your least active days. One benefit of doing this is that you won't compromise your ability to do things on your busiest days because of a lack of energy. Another benefit is fasting for 24 hours can be much easier when you do it on the days when your physical activities are at their lowest.

There's also a workaround to over-cutting your total weekly calories because of not eating for 24 hours twice weekly. To make sure you achieve your weekly calories and deficit, simply distribute the calories of your two fasting days to the five normal eating days. That way, you'll still be able to achieve your weekly caloric goals en route to losing excess body fat.

If your total weekly caloric consumption for losing weight is 14,000 calories, that means a daily caloric intake of 2,000 calories. Not eating anything for two days means an excess caloric deficit of 4,000 calories for the week, which is too much if the primary goal is to focus on losing body fat and not just weight. You can distribute the 4000 calories across your five eating days. So instead of consuming just 2,000 calories daily for five days, you can add 800 calories more on those days. This means consuming 2,800 calories daily for five days every week, which still totals 14,000 calories by the end of the week.

While one advantage of this protocol is moderation, meaning you can eat anything you want as long as they are in moderate amounts, this is not something you can enjoy as part of the endomorph diet. Remember that to lose weight and keep it off, we can't just drastically cut calories, hoping to speed up the process. That's why an integral part of the endomorph diet is estimating the number of calories you need to consume daily given your physical activity level.

The problem with moderation is that it's a highly subjective term, especially in the context of Eat-Stop-Eat. How much is enough? With no objective benchmarks, it's easy to subconsciously justify half a dozen donuts in one sitting as moderate. While that's an exaggeration, the point is your risks of exceeding the required daily caloric intake are very high with this approach.

It's also important to remember that you need to get the proper macronutrient ratios more than simply calculating the total number of daily calories. Because of this, you need to modify this protocol to supplement your endomorph diet using this protocol. You can eat anything, but the amounts will have to be adjusted accordingly.

For example, you can eat donuts during your endomorph diet, but you can't eat them all the time. On the rare times you do, one donut should be enough to minimize the risks of ruining your weight loss progress. Limit cheat foods like these to – at the most – three servings during the week. Otherwise, you'll compromise your ability to lose excess body fat effectively and safely.

The only benefit you can enjoy using this IF protocol to supplement your endomorph diet is limiting your fasting days to just two a week. However, those two fasting days involve complete food fasts for 24 hours each. Fasting daily for justice 14 or 16 hours is much more practical and doable for most people. Hence, the Eat-Stop-Eat protocol isn't an ideal one to use with the endomorph diet.

The Warrior Diet

This protocol is probably the most unique among the popular ones for several reasons.

First, it imitates the way ancient warriors supposedly ate. How? Ori Hofmekler, the Warrior Diet's creator, says that ancient warriors typically ate up to two big meals only and *within a four-hour window* in the evening. You must fast for 20 hours a day with a feeding window of only four hours. I don't know about you, but that sounds kind of tough to pull off regularly.

However, it's still one of the four most popular protocols among dieters despite the very long fasting period, which is practically the whole day and night. It's because of this protocol's second unique characteristic; its different definition of *fasting*.

Fasting refers to intentionally avoiding food for extended periods. But under the warrior diet, fasting isn't that strict because you can eat small amounts of specific types of food within the 20-hour fasting period. Under the protocol, eating small servings of raw vegetables, lean proteins, and fruit is permitted while "fasting."

Yes, you read that right. You can eat while fasting. Just remember your food choices are minimal, and so are the amounts. I suspect this is the primary way dieters quiet their complaining stomachs during the relatively long daily fasts!

Whether or not the great warriors from centuries ago ate this way isn't relevant for losing weight using this protocol. What's important is that it is one of the most popular ways of fasting intermittently because many people swear that they could successfully lose excess weight through this diet.

The only benefit of this intermittent fasting protocol is you won't have to deal with hunger pangs during your fasting hours. Because you can eat small amounts of raw vegetables, fruits, and lean protein throughout the day, and you won't have to deal with a grumbling stomach.

As for the challenges, there is one you should seriously consider: you must eat all your daily calories in just one or two big meals at night. I don't know about you, but stuffing yourself with too much food in just one or two sittings can be very uncomfortable, if not unsustainable.

Just like with the other protocols, there is a workaround for this. Again, you don't have to hit the ground running when it comes to fasting. Hence, you can start your daily "fast" by skipping breakfast first and, instead, eat small portions of either lean protein, raw vegetables, or fruit when you can't stand the hunger anymore. Simultaneously, you can eat your breakfast calories together with dinner. Once you get accustomed to this, you can skip lunch and continue eating small portions of the allowed foods and transferring your lunch calories to dinner. If eating all your daily calories during dinner feels too much, you can split it into two or three smaller meals that you'll eat within a four-hour window.

However, incorporating this into your endomorph diet may not be optimal for you. Why? One reason for incorporating intermittent fasting into your endomorph diet is its ability to improve your insulin sensitivity and promote increased production of fat-burning hormones like human growth hormone and norepinephrine.

But because you're allowed to eat during your 20-hour fasting periods, you will likely trigger your pancreas to produce insulin, regardless of the small amount of food. As a result, you may not maximize the benefits of intermittent fasting regarding improving insulin sensitivity. As an endomorph who is likely to be more insulin dominant, this is very important.

As a result, the warrior diet isn't an ideal supplement to the endomorph diet. It may also not be a practical one because you must eat all of your calories at night within a four-hour window – becoming detrimental to your social or family life. With a tiny eating window, it's hard to share meals with family and friends without breaking the diet.

The Verdict

LeanGains is the ideal intermittent fasting method to supplement your endomorph diet. It's actually a fast, its fasting hours are more realistic, and it provides flexibility in scheduling both fasting and feeding. While you'll need to fast every day, your fasting periods won't be as long as those of Eat-Stop-Eat. This increases the likelihood you can sustain the practice.

And while you're not allowed to eat anything during your 14-or 16-hour daily fasts, you have a much longer time to consume your daily calories. Instead of stuffing yourself with food in just four hours right before going to bed, you have an eight-hour window to get your calories in. It's much easier to sustain a diet that doesn't require you to eat your daily requirements in just one or two meals.

Practical Tips for Starting IF

Before you begin fasting intermittently, remember that doing everything simultaneously increases your risks of being overwhelmed, overstressed, and quitting. That is why instead of going full speed ahead, it's better to do it one step at a time. Specifically, I highly recommend starting with the endomorph diet first. Believe me when I say that strictly counting calories and ensuring you eat the correct number for each macronutrient can feel very tedious, especially initially.

Most people, including you, probably, base the amount of food they eat on how they feel. The right amount makes you feel full, which is neither objective nor consistent. To maximize your chances of successfully losing excess weight, mainly body fat, counting calories isn't an option. Hence, you need first to develop the habit of counting your daily calories.

Once you've got the habit down and can consistently accomplish your daily caloric goals, you can incorporate intermittent fasting into your strategy. Because you're already used to eating relatively strictly, you can devote most of your willpower to developing the habit of fasting for 14 or 16 hours a day.

By starting your endomorph diet first, then adding intermittent fasting, the change to your eating habits won't be so taxing on your mind, emotions, and body. Thus, you can optimize your chances of successfully using both diets and shed those unwanted pounds. But if you start both simultaneously, you'll likely spread yourself too thin and eventually quit.

Another critical thing to remember as you start fasting intermittently is to stay well hydrated by drinking plenty of water throughout the day. More than just hydration, drinking lots of water can help you feel fuller for longer and help make the daily fasts much more bearable.

It's best to schedule your fast, so it starts early in the evening. This way, a big chunk of your fasting hours will fall within your sleeping time. This gives you a big head start because you're already used to fasting while sleeping at night. Technically, you only need to add eight more hours of fasting daily, assuming you get 8 hours of sleep every night.

Finally, exercise is crucial to ensure most of your weight loss is body fat and that you minimize muscle mass loss. For this, the best types of exercises are resistance training and high-intensity interval training or HIIT. We'll talk more about this in the next chapter but suffice to say; you should schedule your workouts within your feeding window. This ensures you have enough energy to perform the right exercises with the required duration and repetitions/sets. Exercising in a fasted state will compromise your ability to properly exercise and, worse, put you at risk for getting injured due to lack of energy or strength.

Chapter 6: Exercise Tips, Guides, and Plans for the Endomorph's Weight Loss Journey

Even if your TDEE increases as you up the ante on your daily physical activity level, incorporating the right kind of regular exercises can help you lose the right kind of weight and, more important, keep it off in the long run.

If you perform the appropriate kinds of exercises regularly, you can prevent your metabolism from slowing down. You can also maintain or even increase muscle mass, which is one of the primary factors determining your BMR, which helps you look much better when you lose weight. Particularly with resistance or strength training and HIIT, you can tone or shape your muscles and look fit.

To give you a better perspective on why you need to incorporate regular exercise into your endomorph diet, I'll give two examples of people able to lose weight; one who only dieted and another who dieted and exercised regularly.

My friend Ryan has always struggled with his weight. He would lose weight only to gain it back after a short while. Every time he wanted to shed unwanted pounds, he went on extreme diets. And each time, he would lose considerable weight.

However, he didn't bother to exercise. Not because he's lazy but because of the nature of his work and his relatively long daily commutes. He felt that incorporating regular exercise into his daily schedule meant cutting into his already shortened sleeping hours. And since extreme diets did help him lose weight every time, he felt justified in skipping the regular exercise part.

Another friend, Joseph, is in the same boat as Ryan - he also struggled with his weight. But he took a different track to lose weight and keeping it off. Instead of relying on extreme diets alone, he counted his calories, paid attention to his daily macronutrient ratios, regularly lifted weights, and did cardio. In short, he emulated professional fitness competitors like bodybuilders to shed excess body fat and weight.

Both Ryan and Joseph lost a considerable amount of weight, but both look different afterward. After losing 10 pounds, Ryan looks frail, and if you didn't personally know him, you would get the impression he may be sick. But Joseph looked fitter and stronger - not to mention thinner - even when he lost one pound less than Ryan.

In short, weight loss didn't look good on Ryan, but it did on Joseph. Why is that so?

The first reason is the kind of diet used to lose excess weight. Ryan used extreme diets known to be unhealthy and ineffective in the long run. Because extreme diets severely cut calories or specific macronutrients, a big chunk of lost weight comprises muscle mass.

A significant decline in muscle mass doesn't just slow down your metabolism and result in weight loss plateaus. It can also make you look frail and weak because of a significant loss of muscle tone. And if you lose more muscle than body fat, you'll look even softer. This is often called looking "skinny-fat," meaning you can look smaller but have high body fat levels.

Another reason for the stark difference in appearance is regular exercise, particularly resistance or strength training exercises. The most apparent benefit of lifting weights or performing bodyweight exercises like calisthenics or TRX is well-toned muscles. When you have them, you look fitter and more robust.

Another significant benefit of exercising regularly is muscle mass preservation. Particularly with resistance or strength training exercises, it's even possible to gain modest amounts of muscle mass. Not only can you burn more calories in the long run via faster metabolism, but you can also look healthier and stronger.

As evident from the examples of Ryan and Joseph, you can burn more body fat if you incorporate regular exercise into your weight loss routine instead of merely relying on diet alone. This is especially true as an endomorph because, remember, one characteristic of this somatotype is a slower metabolism. When you exercise regularly, especially if you do resistance or high-intensity interval training (HIIT), you can speed up your metabolism and accelerate fat loss results. Not only that, but it will also make it easier for you to keep the excess weight you've lost off.

Resistance or Strength Training Exercises

These exercises involve pushing or pulling against a resisting force and, in the process, help increase strength and build muscle mass. Studies have shown that compared to steady-state cardio exercises, which were all the rage in the '80s and part of the '90s, resistance training burns more calories. More importantly, this kind of exercise has a more substantial and more extended afterburn effect. This means even after you've finished working out, your metabolism remains elevated for up to 24 hours, so you continue burning more body fat even while resting.

Lifting weights or performing calisthenic-type exercises is also more practical compared to regular cardio. Because lifting weights burns more calories and body fat, you need not exercise for long periods regularly just to see the weight come off. For significant calorie and fat burn, you must perform steady-state cardio for up to an hour. To burn the same amount, you can do resistance training workouts in under 30 minutes.

Not that steady-state cardio exercises are worthless. When used wisely, they can maximize the fat-burning effects of your resistance training sessions. However, you shouldn't use it as your primary exercise of choice for optimal fat burning.

Another reason for prioritizing resistance or strength training workouts is the ability to preserve and build muscle mass. Remember that because muscles are the most metabolically active cells in the body, increasing your muscle mass can lead to faster resting metabolism rates. Your body can burn more calories and body fat even while at rest.

But your metabolism may slow down if you lose significant muscle mass during the weight loss process. This is why we continue to emphasize fat loss more than just general weight loss. Since this type of exercise can help preserve or minimize muscle mass loss, you can stave off weight loss plateaus.

With resistance training, you must focus on performing compound exercises. These involve multiple joints and body parts, and their movements recruit multiple muscle groups. The more muscles are involved, the more calories and body fat are burned, making compound resistance training exercises very effective for losing body fat and can help you save a lot of time.

The four compound exercises you should include in your strength-training regimen are squats, deadlifts, overhead press, and bench press.

Squats

Squats are considered the king of weightlifting exercises - and for a good reason.

First, it's the complete exercise for building total-body strength. Doing it regularly and properly leads to better overall athletic performance, especially in sports that require explosive movements like jumping or running.

Squatting involves the use of most muscle groups, primarily the biggest one - your legs. The primary leg muscles involved in the movement are your thighs or quadricep muscles, glute muscles, your hamstrings, and to some extent, your calves.

It also requires balancing and stabilizing your upper body, especially if you're squatting with a barbell hoisted on your shoulders. Doing this also helps strengthen your core and lower back muscles. Since the barbell is hoisted on your upper body, you also recruit your upper back, shoulder, and chest muscles to stabilize the weight.

No wonder it's the king of all strength and muscle-building exercises.

And since we're on the topic of losing weight (particularly body fat), squats are indispensable to your workout routine. Considering that the primary muscles involved are your legs, which are the biggest muscle group in your body, squats burn the most calories and, by extension, body fat.

Because it also involves other muscle groups, the caloric and body fat burn is maximized. Hence, you become stronger, maintain muscle mass, and burn more body fat.

Another significant benefit of performing squats regularly is improved stability, mobility, and lower body strength. Together, these can help you minimize your risks for accidental falls and related injuries. It also helps you minimize your risks of getting injured when lifting things off the ground or carrying heavy items.

And last – but certainly not least – regular squatting with weights can give you solid glutes and a defined waistline. More than just burning the most body fat (one of the essential components of looking fit and toned), squatting primarily works out your butt muscles and gives your core muscles excellent training. As a result, you can naturally increase your butt muscle mass and achieve a nice, round set of buns. By providing much-needed torso support, your core muscles can become much tighter and toner.

The traditional squat involves placing a barbell on your traps and shoulders and squatting until your thighs and hamstrings are parallel to the floor before rising back up. This emphasizes your butt and thigh muscles, with your hamstrings and calves providing stability and support.

To shift the emphasis more onto other leg muscles, such as your hamstrings, you can change things up by adopting a much wider leg stance. Squatting at shoulder or hip-width emphasizes your thighs are quads.

Another squatting variety involves placing the barbell on top of your front shoulders and crossing your arms beneath it for support. Squatting this way puts most, if not all, of the load on your thighs or quads. Your butt or glute muscles simply provide necessary stability and support with the hamstrings.

Finally, you can also try different squatting techniques using different pieces of equipment. Other than a barbell, you can use dumbbells, kettlebells, a Smith machine, resistance bands, or other heavy objects. But if you're new to resistance or weightlifting training, the best place to start is with a barbell.

With any strength training exercise, you must prioritize proper form, and squats are no different. Don't lift heavier weights than you can handle without proper form. If you lift heavy and use an incorrect or sloppy form, you'll put yourself at significant risk of getting injured.

The improper form also robs you of the opportunity to maximize the number of calories and the body fat you can burn while working out. Without correct form, you won't correctly move the weight throughout its effective range of motion – and you be able to maximize the number of calories burned.

So, prioritize proper form over heavy weights. Your ability to execute the movements properly should determine how heavy you can lift and not the other way around.

Here's the proper way to perform a traditional barbell squat:

1. Place yourself beneath the barbell on a squat rack. Let your traps and shoulders press firmly beneath the bar and hold both sides of the barbell with your hands.

2. Keep your lower back straight and bring your hips as far back as possible.

3. Push upward with your legs to lift the barbell off the rack and pick a step or two away so you can start squatting.

4. Bring your body down by bending at the hips and the knees while keeping your lower back straight throughout the exercise. This is crucial to avoid injuring your lower back.

5. When your thighs and hamstrings are parallel to the ground, stop. Also, make sure that your knees never go past your toes at any point during the squat to minimize risks for knee injuries.

6. Push the weight back up with your legs by pushing through your heels. Don't let your legs straighten entirely to the point that your knee joints lock. Instead, stop short of locking out. This prevents your knee joints from bearing the barbell's weight and ensures continuous tension in your thighs and glute muscles to maximize the exercise's beneficial effects. This completes one repetition.

7. Perform two to three sets of 10 to 12 repetitions each.

Deadlifts

Second only to the squat, deadlifts also work on multiple muscle groups simultaneously. These are the legs, back, and core muscles, and it also works out your forearms as you grip the barbell throughout the movements.

For the leg muscles, deadlifts work out the hamstrings or the leg muscles behind your thighs and directly below your butt. When it comes to the back muscles, it primarily works out your lower back and, to some extent, the middle of your back. Together, these two muscle groups comprise most muscles in your body, so performing deadlifts also burns a lot of calories and body fat. It also helps you increase overall body strength.

Another vital benefit of regularly performing deadlifts is reduced risks of lower back injuries. More than just strengthening your lower back muscles, learning to perform this exercise using proper form minimizes your risks of lower back injuries from simply picking things up from the floor. Many people injure their lower back after picking up a pen from the floor because they arch their lower back when doing so. As a regular deadlifter, keeping your back straight while bending down becomes a habit for you.

As with the squats, you can perform deadlifts in various ways using different pieces of equipment other than a barbell. You can use dumbbells, machines, resistance bands, or even a heavy pail of water. Using a barbell, you also have a choice of using overhand grips or alternate ones, with one hand holding the barbell in a pronated position while the other does so in a supinated position.

Here's how to perform deadlifts correctly using the traditional way, i.e., a barbell:

1. Stand behind the barbell placed on the floor and assume a narrow leg stance.

2. Bend forward at the waist, ensuring you keep your lower back straight and slightly bending at the knees to grip the barbell with your hands at the shoulder width interval.

3. Before you lift the barbell off the floor, make sure your lower back is straight, your hips are down, and your shoulders are directly above your knees to avoid getting injured.

4. Gripping the barbell tightly, straighten up your body and legs to lift the barbell off the floor. At the top of this movement, the barbell should be pressing against the front of your hips or crotch area. Always remember to keep your lower back straight.

5. Begin to lower the barbell back to the floor in a slow and controlled movement by bending at the waist and slightly bending your knees. That completes one repetition.

6. Perform two to three sets of 10 to 12 repetitions each.

Overhead Presses

Also called military or shoulder presses, this compound strength training exercise works out your shoulder muscles. Specifically, it helps strengthen and grow your front shoulders or delts. As the name implies, the movement involves pushing weight above your head, which primarily activates your front deltoids and triceps muscles.

There are two general ways to perform the overhead press; seated and standing. But to burn more calories, standing overhead presses are recommended because you can recruit more muscles.

When you perform seated overhead presses, you work out the leg muscles in the process. And if you perform them while sitting on an incline or upright bench to support your back, you also work out your lower back muscles.

When you perform overhead presses standing up, you engage your legs, lower back, and core muscles for balance and stability. As a result, you can burn more calories compared to performing the exercise seated on a bench.

You can perform this exercise using a variety of equipment. For optimal fat burning and muscle building, barbell overhead presses are the top choice. But if you don't have access to a barbell or your physical condition restricts you from using one, you can use a pair of dumbbells, kettlebells, a smith machine press, or even resistance bands.

When performing standing overhead presses, lift the maximum weight that allows you to use proper form in every repetition. If you're not able to do it, it's a red flag that you're lifting too much weight. Reduce the weight so that you strike a balance between effectively working out your muscles and safety.

More than just being one of the most effective at burning compound exercises, performing standing overhead presses regularly helps you develop greater functional strength. This can help you lift heavy objects above your head with greater ease.

It also helps you develop a stronger core. This can help you perform various daily movements and reduce your risks of lower back and other related injuries.

Overhead standing presses are also an excellent complement to your bench press. Why?

First, this exercise helps you strengthen and grow your triceps. Strong triceps are essential for doing heavy bench presses.

The other reason it's a perfect complement to bench pressing is that strong front shoulders are necessary for stabilizing the barbell or dumbbells while performing free-weight bench presses. Since the exercise primarily strengthens and builds up your front deltoids, it can indirectly contribute to your bench press progress.

Finally, this exercise can help improve your athletic performance across various sports activities by training your core muscles at an anti-extension angle. In layman's terms, standing overhead presses help you develop strength around your midsection, from your abdominals to your side obliques and lower back.

Why is this supremely beneficial? Developing strength across all muscles in your midsection minimizes your risks of overextending your lower back or side obliques in one direction during sports activities like football, basketball, tennis, and soccer. Hence the term *anti-extension.*

Performing the exercise is very simple. However, don't let its simplicity lull you into complacency. Always use proper form to minimize your risks of lower back injuries. Here's how to do it properly and safely:

1. Before you start, make sure that the barbell is securely placed on the rack at a height that's approximately level with your chin. Wear a weightlifting belt if one is available.

2. Grip the barbell with hands at shoulder-width apart.

3. Stand very close to the barbell with your upper chest beneath the barbell.

4. Plant your feet firmly on the ground at shoulder width or slightly shoulder-width apart, depending on how stable you feel.

5. Lift the barbell above your head by pressing it upward and driving your heels to the ground. At the top of the movement, don't let your elbows lock out at full extension. Instead, stop short of locking out to prevent your elbow joints from bearing the weight of the barbell. Doing this also ensures you maintain continuous tension on your shoulder and triceps muscles, which is essential for optimizing your strength and muscle-building training.

6. In a slow and controlled manner, lower the barbell until it's in line with your chin. This completes one repetition.

7. Perform two to three sets of 10 to 12 repetitions each.

8. Carefully place the barbell back on the rack at the end of each set.

When performing overhead standing presses, always keep your lower back straight and be mindful of not overextending it. Wearing a weightlifting belt can help you develop this habit.

Bench Presses

The last of the essential compound strength training exercises, this exercise builds and strengthens the chest muscles. Much like squats and overhead presses, you can perform this in various ways so you can target specific areas of this muscle group.

For example, performing bench presses on a flat bench will work out more of your middle chest area. If you perform bench presses on an incline platform, you can focus more on your upper chest. Performed on a decline bench, the emphasis is placed on the lower pectoral muscles.

You can also perform this using a variety of equipment. Besides the traditional barbell press, you can use a pair of dumbbells, a Smith machine press, machine bench presses, or resistance bands. But for optimal muscle building and fat burning, the best version is still the barbell bench press. Incorporating bench presses as part of your regular strength training routine helps you build more strength and power, critical factors in your overall fitness level.

If you're into running, bench presses can also help you run faster. How? Performing bench presses properly helps you build upper body strength and muscular endurance, which play an essential role in terms of efficient running. Regularly bench pressing helps you develop a natural, forward-looking posture and steady torso. These are important components of proper running form.

Also, arm swings are an integral part of the optimal running motion. Believe it or not, your chest muscles are involved when you swing your arms alternately as you run. The optimal running form requires synchronized arm swings and leg strides. For your arm swings to keep up with your leg speed, your chest muscles need to have adequate strength and endurance.

As with all types of strength training or weightlifting exercises, proper form is necessary. Here's how to perform bench presses the right way:

1. Assume the starting position by lying on the bench with your eyes directly beneath the barbell.

2. Grip the barbell with your hands at shoulder width or slightly wider than shoulder-width apart. Your thumbs should be over your other fingers instead of beside them for the best and safest grip.

3. Draw your shoulders back, plant your feet firmly on the ground, and tighten your core muscles as you begin.

4. Push the barbell up and move it above your chest.

5. In a slow and controlled manner, lower the barbell until your elbows are at a 90-degree angle or until your upper arms are parallel to the ground.

6. Push the barbell back up in a controlled manner (no jerking movements) and stop just short of your elbows locking out. Don't let your elbows lock out at the top of the movement because doing so places the barbell's weight mostly on your elbow joints and puts them at risk of injury.

7. This completes one repetition. Perform up to three sets of 10 to 12 repetitions each.

8. Always remember to keep your shoulders drawn back throughout the movement. This prevents your front shoulders from assisting your chest in pushing the weight up. Remember, your front shoulders must only provide stability and support. It's not meant to help your chest push the weight up.

Working Out

Now that you're familiar with the most essential compound strength training exercises, it's time to structure a workout routine. Because these require weights like a barbell or a pair of dumbbells, you'll most likely have to work out in a gym.

One of the most important things to consider for choosing and implementing the workout routine is training frequency. To maximize muscle recovery, give your muscles at least 48 hours of rest before the next strength training or weightlifting workout. If you trained chest on a Monday, your next chest workout should be on Wednesday at the earliest.

This is often one of the most neglected aspects of strength training. People think that working out the same muscle groups every day will help them become stronger and bigger much faster. However, lifting weights is just one-third of the equation. The other two critical components are rest and nutrition. By letting at least 48 hours pass before your next workout, you'll give your muscles enough rest so they will be fully recovered on the next workout.

For an optimal fat-burning workout routine, consider workout sessions that include all four compound strength training exercises. To work out frequently using this routine, just make sure you do it every other day to give your body at least 48 hours of recuperation time. A good workout schedule is Monday, Wednesday, and Friday. You can also schedule a workout every Monday, Thursday, and Saturday. The important thing is to get at least three workouts per week with 48 hours of rest between each.

Here's how a typical workout session could look like:

• Warm-up for 15 minutes with steady-state cardio, e.g., stationary biking or brisk walking on a treadmill.

• Perform three sets of barbell squats for 10 to 12 repetitions each.

- Perform three sets of barbell deadlifts for 10 to 12 repetitions each.

- Perform three sets of barbell or dumbbell for 10 to 12 repetitions each.

- Perform three sets of barbell bench presses for 10 to 12 repetitions each.

- Finish the workout with 20-minute cardio activity, e.g., stationary biking or brisk walking on a treadmill.

For maximum fat burning effect, keep your resting periods between sets no more than 30 seconds. Doing this helps keep your heart rate as elevated as possible to continue burning more calories and body fat even while resting between sets.

TRX Workouts

Also called *suspension training*, TRX stands for Total Body Resistance Exercise. This type of resistance or strength training is also called *calisthenics*, which uses a person's body weight as resistance instead of weights like barbells and dumbbells. TRX workouts can help you develop joint stability, core strength, flexibility, balance, coordination, and, more importantly, strength and muscle mass in ways relatively safer compared to weightlifting.

Another reason for the popularity of TRX workouts is flexibility. Compared to traditional strength training exercises at the gym, you only need a suspension trainer to perform countless strength and muscle-building exercises. It's a very sturdy set of exercise straps that you can anchor at the top of any stable door, overhead bar, or wall-mounted brace. It's also very portable because you can simply roll it up, put it in a small pouch bag, and you can take it anywhere you go. Investing in this type of exercise equipment gives you the benefit of getting your resistance training workouts in even while you're on an out-of-town vacation.

Strength training using the TRX system can give you several benefits. One of them is simplicity. Because you use the same piece of equipment for all your suspension training exercises, you don't waste time transitioning from one exercise to another. You can practically go from exercising one body part to another in a matter of seconds. The only thing you may need to change is the length adjustment of the straps, depending on the next exercise.

Another key benefit to using TRX for resistance training is strengthening and building endurance for your core muscles. Ultimately, it can help you shrink your waistline quicker compared to other exercise programs. You'll work out your core muscles in practically all the exercises on the TRX suspension trainer. And more than just looking thinner with a smaller and tighter waistline, you can also look fitter and more muscular because well-developed core muscles allow you to stand with much better posture.

But more than just aesthetics, stronger core muscles help you minimize risks for exercise and sports-related injuries. Some benefits of having a solid set of core muscles are greater stability and balance, both of which help reduce your risks of accidental falls and muscle strains.

The ability to customize your training level is another benefit of TRX training. You can easily adjust the resistance level, which is the equivalent of weighted plates at the gym, by simply adjusting the straps' length and the angle at which you perform exercises. Doing this helps you to adjust the bodyweight you work with for each exercise.

Working out with suspension straps also helps you develop excellent body balance. As the name implies, working out with a TRX training system involves suspending your body above the ground via the straps. To properly execute the movements involved in every exercise, you must stabilize and balance your body. With consistent workouts, you can learn how to balance your body much better.

As simple as it seems, working out using a TRX suspension system isn't that easy. With traditional strength training or weightlifting exercises, you need not exert much effort to balance your body. It's because you'll only be working against one-directional resistance.

Barbell squats, for example, require working or pushing against downward resistance produced by the weight of the barbell. There is minimal or no push or pull resistance at the sides, front, or back with proper form.

Because you're suspending your body weight using straps, you'll be working with multi-directional resistance. When performing a chest press using the TRX suspension trainer, for example, you're not just working against a downward angled resistance. You'll also have to deal with sideward resistance to stay balanced throughout the pressing movement. This can be much challenging than simply hoisting weights up and down.

That's why when you start training with the TRX suspension system, you must first learn to use proper form and technique by focusing on the basic exercises first. Only after you've developed good balancing and stabilizing skills should you proceed with more advanced or complicated exercises.

Since you'll be working primarily with body weight, the chances are high that you'll need to compensate for the limited resistance levels with more repetitions and sets. Ideally, go for three to five sets of 12 to 15 repetitions each. If you're not able to do at least 12 repetitions, reduce the resistance level by shortening the strap's length or adjusting the angle of your body closer to a 90-degree angle from the floor.

Because all exercises require balancing your body and maintaining a tight core, every exercise is practically a compound one that involves several muscle groups at a time, whether directly or indirectly. As such, TRX workouts can help you burn lots of calories and body fat without having to work out for over 30 minutes.

Like traditional strength training or weightlifting workouts, it's best to keep rest periods between sets short. Ideally, keep it to no more than 30 seconds.

You must also give your muscles enough recovery time. Give your muscles at least 48 hours of rest before the next workout.

There are so many excellent fat-burning exercises you can do with TRX suspension trainers. Detailed instructions for them all come with the equipment.

High-Intensity Interval Training

Also called HIIT, it's a type of exercise that involves quick bursts of intense exercise alternating with recovery periods of low-intensity activities. Most experts agree that HIIT is probably the most time-efficient way to work out.

HIIT sessions may vary in duration. For a beginner, it may be as short as 5 to 10 minutes only. For the more seasoned ones, it could range from 15 to 30 minutes. Regardless of how long or short your workouts are, you can enjoy health benefits comparable two twice as you can get from longer-duration moderate-intensity exercises.

You can perform HIIT in a variety of ways. You can use a stationary bike, sprint outdoors, or perform many calisthenic or bodyweight exercises like burpees. You can even use weights or TRX suspension trainers to do HIIT. The important thing here is to exercise at high and low intensities alternately.

A typical HIIT protocol can involve 30 seconds of all-out physical activity followed by 30 seconds of low-intensity movement. For example, you can run at an all-out sprint for 30 seconds and then walk for the next 30 to complete one cycle. You can repeat this cycle several times in your workout. Typically, HIIT practitioners perform anywhere from 4 to 8 repetitions per workout at the minimum.

Why should you consider HIIT as part of your endomorph diet weight loss strategy? There are several good reasons to do so.

First, you can burn more calories – and body fat – in a shorter amount of time. On average, HIIT can burn up to 30% more calories and body fat compared to other forms of exercise, according to a published PubMed study. You can burn the same body fat after other forms of exercise, but you need not exercise as long every time. That's why high-intensity interval training is the ideal fat loss exercise strategy for very busy people.

Another key benefit of doing HIIT is the ability to continue burning calories or body fat at a higher rate even after working out. According to a PubMed published study, HIIT elevates your metabolism even after working out, so the post-workout calorie burn is much higher than running and lifting weights. More importantly, the post-workout burn involves mainly body fat rather than carbohydrates. This means you continue burning body fat long after you're done exercising. As a result, HIIT can help you lose more body fat compared to other forms of exercise.

The fat-burning benefits don't end there. With high-intensity interval training, you may even possibly build some muscle, according to several studies. Because muscles are the most metabolically active cells in the body, more muscle mass means a faster metabolism and more calories or body fat burning. However, most of the muscle mass increase recorded in these studies was in the trunk and leg areas due to the specific HIIT exercises.

Another significant benefit of HIIT training – one especially helpful to endomorphs – is its ability to improve insulin resistance. Remember, one of the significant reasons you quickly gain weight and have a challenging time losing it is being insulin-dominant.

A summary of 50 studies on HIIT found that not only does this type of training help bring down blood sugar levels, it also improves insulin resistance much better compared to other traditional types of regular exercise. Not only can it help you address one of the main reasons for gaining and keeping weight as an endomorph, but it can also help you reduce your risks of diabetes.

Lastly, another great reason to consider HIIT for regular exercise in the endomorph diet plan is *practicality.* You can perform high-intensity interval training exercises using a variety of implements or none. If you love to bike, you can do cycling HIITs. If you prefer walking outdoors, you can alternate sprints and walking breaks for interval training. If it's raining and you prefer to stay indoors, you can perform bodyweight (calisthenic) exercises for HIIT, too. With high-intensity interval training, the only reasons you cannot have exercise regularly are laziness and sickness.

What's Your Intensity Level?

Before starting, you must be familiar with the term "high intensity." This is key to making the training work for you to burn excess body fat and achieve your goals.

How can you tell if you're exercising at high intensity? You can do it two ways: using a watch with a heart rate monitor and using the talk test.

Since the more precise way of determining your current exercise intensity is through heartrate monitoring, let's start using a heartrate monitor-equipped watch first. You'll first need to know what your maximum heart rate (MHR) is. The formula for that is:

Your Maximum Heart rate = 220 – Your Age

If you're 40 years old, then your maximum heart rate is 180 beats-per-minute (BPM). If you're 20 years old, it's 200 BPM.

For training at high intensity, your heart rate should be between 70% and 90% of your MHR. Going back to our earlier examples, if you're 40 years old, your heart rate while exercising should be between 126 BPM and 162 BPM. If you're 20 years old with an MHR of 200 BPM, you're training at high intensity when your heart rate is between 140 BPM (70%) and 180 BPM (90%).

If you don't have a gadget that can measure your heart rate, or if you suspect it's inaccurate, you can do it manually. After performing the high-intensity phase of an exercise, use a finger or two to take your pulse for 10 seconds. Multiply the number of pulses you get by 6, and you have your current heart rate.

A much easier yet relatively accurate way of checking your current intensity level is the talk test. Try to talk like you're in a conversation with a friend immediately after the high-intensity part of the interval. If you can speak normally with no to catch your breath, then that's low-intensity training. If you can speak normally, although with some strain in your breathing, that's medium or mid-intensity. If you can barely talk because you need to catch your breath, that's high intensity.

Getting Started With HIIT

Fortunately, starting a HIIT regimen is neither complicated nor impractical. You can choose from various exercises that you can alternate high and low-intensity intervals. These include:

- Running/Sprinting
- Biking
- Bodyweight Exercises or Calisthenics
- Strength/Resistance Training

Regardless of your choice of exercise, warm up first before doing HIIT. Not only can it help you perform better, but it also reduces your risks of injuries, as doing so helps limber up your muscles. Considering you'll be going all out from the get-go, this is crucial to keep you injury-free.

You can do any steady-state cardio for at least 15 minutes to warm up, followed by dynamic stretches. A dynamic stretch is simply performing the featured exercise at a very low intensity or pace, i.e., if you plan to make sprints, walk briskly to warm up. If it's cycling, bike at a leisurely pace. Once you're adequately warmed up, you can start your HIIT.

As a beginner, start with a 20/10 interval first, i.e., 20-second high-intensity burst followed by a 10-second low-intensity break. Perform ten intervals (approximately 5 minutes).

After you complete the ten intervals, finish your workout by performing steady-state cardio for 15 to 20 minutes. According to fitness guru Shaun Hadsall, creator of best-selling fat loss program Over 40 Ab Solution and 4 Cycle Fat Loss Solution, this serves as a flushing mechanism for the fat cells released by your body during HIIT. That is why bodybuilders finish their workouts with steady-state cardio when cutting for bodybuilding shows.

To maximize your HIIT fat loss, avoid eating anything within 1 hour after you finish the workout. According to Hadsall, doing this forces your body to continue burning more body fat after working out and maximizes your weight loss.

Once you've become accustomed to a 20/10 interval, you can take it a notch further to 30/30. This time perform eight intervals, which should take you 8 minutes to finish. Once you're accustomed to it, go for a 60/60 split for 8 to 10 intervals.

That's it! I told you it was easy and practical! If you prefer running, sprint as hard as you can during high-intensity intervals and brisk walk during the low-intensity ones. If you like to bike, pedal as hard and as fast as possible during high-intensity intervals and alternate it with a low-intensity, leisurely pace. To lift weights, go for compound exercises – preferably squats – and use enough weight that you reach failure at the end of the high-intensity intervals. For the low-intensity intervals, you can walk or rest.

But if you prefer to do HIIT from the comfort of your own home, nothing beats bodyweight exercises. You need no equipment to perform them. Here are some of the best calisthenic exercises you can do for HIIT at home and how to do them.

Burpees

1. Begin by squatting with your knees bent and feet approximately shoulder-width apart. Keep your lower back straight.

2. Bring both hands down on the floor inside your feet and in front of you.

3. Resting your body weight on both hands, kick both feet back. You must be in a push-up position after doing it, i.e., you're on your toes and hands.

4. Perform a push-up, keeping your lower back straight and shoulders drawn back.

5. Frog-kick your feet back to their starting position.

6. Stand and raise both arms overhead.

7. Jump as quickly as you can and as you return to the ground, return to the starting position, i.e., squatting and both hands on the ground. This completes one repetition.

8. Perform as many repetitions as you can for the duration of the high-intensity portion of your intervals.

Mountain Climbers

1. Start by going on all fours, i.e., push-up position.

2. Bring your left knee as close as possible to your chest.

3. Using one swift move, switch knees/feet while maintaining your arms' position.

4. With another swift move, switch knees/feet to complete one repetition.

5. Perform as many repetitions as you can for the duration of the high-intensity portion of your intervals.

Bear Crawls

1. Get on all fours while lifting both knees approximately 1 inch off the ground and at a 90-degree angle.

2. Keep your lower back flat at all times to minimize risks for injuries.

3. Keep both legs approximately hip-width apart and your arms about shoulder-width apart.

4. Take a step forward by moving your right hand forward simultaneously with your left foot while maintaining a close-to-the-ground profile.

5. Take another step forward by moving both the left hand and right foot forward, keeping your body close to the ground. This completes one repetition.

6. Perform as many repetitions as you can for the duration of the high-intensity portion of your intervals.

Squat Jumps

1. Begin by standing straight with your feet approximately shoulder-width apart.

2. Perform a regular squat.

3. As your return from the squat, keep your core and lower back straight and jump explosively.

4. Land softly on your forefoot and return to the squatting position. This completes one repetition. Landing on your forefoot ensures a soft landing, while landing on your heels can lead to foot and knee injuries due to the jarring force generated by your falling back to the ground.

5. Perform as many repetitions as you can for the duration of the high-intensity portion of your intervals.

High Knees

1. Start by standing straight with both feet approximately hip-width apart.

2. Sprint in place by lifting one knee as high as possible and alternating it with the other as fast as possible. As you lower your knee, make sure your forefoot hits the ground to soften contact with the ground and minimize risks for heel and knee injuries due to the jarring force of landing on the ground.

3. Perform as many repetitions as you can for the duration of the high-intensity portion of your intervals.

Timing Your Workouts

If you plan to incorporate intermittent fasting with the endomorph diet, timing your workouts is crucial. Ideally, you should do them within your feeding window. Why?

This is to ensure you have enough fuel for a grueling workout, especially when lifting weights. Scheduling them within your feeding window, with at least 1.5 hours before your feeding window ends, allows you to eat your post-workout meal 1 hour after you finish your workout. Remember, this helps you maximize the post-workout fat burn while still feeding your body with much-needed nutrients after exercising.

Chapter 7: Endomorph-Friendly Recipes and Meal Plans

Breakfast Recipes

Veggietatas

Servings: 12

Nutrition per serving:

- Calories: 128
- Fat: 7 grams
- Carbs: 8 grams
- Protein 9.5 grams

Ingredients

- 24 ounces butternut squash, cut into ½ inch dice
- ½ teaspoon salt
- 1 teaspoon smoked paprika
- ½ teaspoon black pepper
- 1 ½ teaspoons crushed rosemary
- ¼ cup grated parmesan cheese

- 16 ounces fresh button mushrooms or cremini mushrooms, thinly sliced
- 4 tablespoons chopped fresh flat-leaf parsley
- 10 egg whites
- 10 eggs
- 6 teaspoons olive oil

Instructions

- Cook butternut squash in a pot of water until tender, making sure not to overcook. Drain off the water and set it aside. Meanwhile, set your oven to broil mode preheat your broiler.
- Cook the butternut squash in 2 teaspoons oil in a large ovenproof skillet (10 – 12 inches diameter) until light brown. Remove the squash from the pan and place it in a bowl.
- Cook mushrooms in 4 teaspoons oil in the same skillet until tender. Stir in crushed rosemary.
- Throw the broccoli and squash in and continue cooking for up to 4 minutes or until the veggies become tender-crispy.
- Whisk the egg whites, whole eggs, salt, pepper, paprika, and parsley in a medium-sized bowl. When done, pour this mixture over the veggies in the skillet and continue cooking on medium heat.
- As the mixture begins to set, run a spatula along the skillet's edge and raise the egg mixture to help ensure even cooking.
- Continue cooking and lifting the mixture's edges until the mixture becomes nearly set.
- Sprinkle cheese on top.
- Transfer the skillet containing the mixture to your pre-heated broiler, place it 4 and 5 inches away from the heat. Broil the mixture for up to 2 minutes or until the cheese has melted and the top has set.

Soft-Boiled Caprese

Servings: 2

Nutrition per serving:

- Calories: 243
- Fat: 27 grams
- Carbs: 7 grams
- Protein: 26 grams

Ingredients

- Kosher salt and freshly ground black pepper to taste
- Fresh basil leaves, chopped to serve
- 6 thin slices (about 2 ounces) of fresh mozzarella
- 4 large eggs
- 2 teaspoons extra-virgin olive oil
- 2 small or medium tomatoes, thinly sliced

Instructions

- Boil a small pot of water, and afterward, lower the eggs in it gently using a ladle or a long-handled spoon. Avoid dropping the eggs because doing so can crack them as they hit the bottom of the pot.
- Reduce the heat to bring the water down to a gentle simmer and continue cooking the eggs in it for 6 minutes.
- Once the eggs are boiled, carefully remove them from the hot water and transfer them to a bowl of ice-cold water or place them under cold running water until they're cool enough to hold.
- Tap each egg gently on a solid surface and gently roll the eggs to crack the shell. Finally, peel off the shells.
- On a serving plate, place the eggs in the center and arrange the tomato slices and mozzarella around them. Drizzle the Caprese with olive oil, season with pepper and salt, sprinkle some basil, and cut the eggs open to let the yolks ooze out.

Bulletproof Coffee

Servings: 1

Nutrition per serving:

- Calories: 280
- Fat: 31 grams
- Carbs: 2.8 grams
- Protein: 1 gram

Ingredients

- ½ scoop Perfect Keto MCT Powder
- 1 cup freshly brewed hot coffee
- ½ teaspoon Ceylon cinnamon
- 1 tablespoon grass-fed butter

Instructions

- Put all the ingredients in your blender or food processor.
- Blend everything at low speed, and after a few seconds, increase the speed too high for up to 30 seconds or until your coffee turns frothy.
- If you enjoy milk in your bulletproof coffee, you may add some heavy cream or unsweetened almond milk for added flavor. Just remember that doing so can add a

Egg Salad

Servings: 2 (½ cup per serving)

Nutrition per serving:

- Calories: 473
- Fat: 45 grams
- Carbs: 1 grams
- Protein: 13 grams

Ingredients

- ½ finely chopped tablespoon chives
- ½ teaspoon lemon juice
- ¼ cup Low Carb mayonnaise
- ¼ teaspoon salt
- 1 teaspoon Dijon mustard
- 4 large eggs
- A pinch of paprika
- 1/8 teaspoon pepper

Instructions

- Pour hot tap water into a saucepan and heat over high heat.
- Carefully submerge the cold eggs in the saucepan.
- As soon as the water boils, let it cook for 12 minutes.
- After boiling the eggs, drain off the water and let them chill in ice or cool water for 10 minutes.
- Once cooled, peel the eggs, cut them into small pieces, and put them in your mixing bowl.
- Mix all the remaining ingredients in and gently stir the mixture. Use additional salt and pepper to taste until you achieve your desired flavor.

• If you don't plan to eat the salad right away, you can store it in an airtight container and keep it in the refrigerator for up to three days.

Skillet Eggs and Chorizo

Servings: 2

Nutrition per serving:

- Calories: 450
- Fat: 33 grams
- Carbs: 13 grams
- Protein: 23 grams

Ingredients

- ½ tablespoon extra-virgin olive oil
- ½ teaspoon chipotle chili flakes
- ¼ pound Mexican chorizo, casings removed
- 1 jalapeño (from a jar), finely chopped
- 1 large handful flat-leaf parsley, roughly chopped
- 1 ounce feta cheese, crumbled
- 1 teaspoon granulated sugar
- 12 garlic cloves, crushed
- 2 large eggs
- Kosher salt and freshly ground black pepper to taste
- Sour cream, to serve (optional)
- 1 can (14-ounces) diced tomatoes

Instructions

- Heat oil in a big skillet set over medium heat. When the oil heats up, throw in the chorizo and break it into tiny bits using a wooden spoon. Cook for about 5 minutes or until the chorizo releases its fat and turns golden brown.

- Stir the jalapeño and continue cooking for about a minute.

- Mix in the garlic and tomatoes and increase the heat to high. Soon the tomatoes will begin to bubble.

- Stir in the chili flakes and sugar and continue cooking for about 5 minutes, allowing the tomatoes to cook until slightly dry. Sprinkle salt and pepper to taste and stir the mixture.
- Create two holes (cavities) in the mixture, and inside each hole, crack an egg. Continue cooking until you see the whites of the eggs are set.
- Garnish the eggs with feta and parsley to enjoy. You may even serve it with a drizzle of sour cream.

Lunch and Dinner Recipes

Chipotle-Style Barbacoa

Servings: 3

Nutrition per serving:

- Calories: 245
- Fat: 14 grams
- Carbs: 7 grams
- Protein: 21 grams

Ingredients

- 1 pound beef chuck roast, trimmed, cut into 3 pieces
- ½ cup chicken broth
- 1 Serrano chili pepper, chopped (optional)
- ½ small onion, finely chopped
- ½ tablespoon ground cayenne pepper, or more to taste (optional)
- ½ teaspoon garlic powder
- ½ teaspoon ground black pepper
- ¼ teaspoon ground cloves
- ½ teaspoon salt
- 3 tablespoons apple cider
- 1 ¼ teaspoons dried oregano
- ½ tablespoon vegetable oil
- 2 small bay leaves
- 1 ½ tablespoons lime juice
- 2 chipotle peppers in adobo sauce
- 2 cloves garlic, peeled, or more to taste
- 2 teaspoons ground cumin

Instructions

- Add oil into a skillet and heat over low heat and gradually raise the heat to medium-high.

- Once the oil is hot, cook the beef chuck pieces until they turn brown or about 10 seconds on each side. When done, turn of the heat and add the beef into your slow cooker.

- In your food processor or blender, throw in the ground cloves, salt, garlic powder, black pepper, oregano, cayenne pepper, Serrano pepper, cumin, garlic, lime juice, chipotle peppers, and apple cider. Blend the ingredients until you achieve a smooth textured mixture and pour it over the beef chunks in the slow cooker.

- Mix in the bay leaves, onion, and chicken broth, stirring them gently into the mixture.

- Set your slow cooker on low for six to eight hours or until the beef chuck becomes tender enough to shred with forks. When done, shred the meat with a pair of forks.

- Add the meat back into the pot. Stir well and serve.

Slow-cooked Shredded Beef in Lettuce Cups

Servings: 4 (3 lettuce cups per)

Nutrition per serving:

- Calories: 270
- Fat: 11 grams
- Carbs: 18 grams
- Protein: 24 grams

Ingredients

- ½ can (from an 8-ounces) unsweetened crushed pineapple, with its liquid
- ½ garlic clove, minced
- ½ medium onion, chopped
- ¼ cup reduced-sodium soy sauce
- ¼ teaspoon pepper
- 1 medium sweet red pepper, chopped
- 1 pound of boneless beef chuck roast
- 1 tablespoon packed brown sugar
- 1 tablespoon white vinegar
- 12 Bibb or Boston lettuce leaves
- 1 ½ medium carrots, peeled and chopped
- 1 ½ tablespoons cornstarch mixed with 1 ½ tablespoons water
- Thinly sliced green onions to garnish

Instructions

- Mix the onion, peppers, carrots, and roast in a slow cooker.
- In a small mixing bowl, combine the remaining ingredients except for the lettuce leaves, water, and corn starch. Once done, pour the mixture over the roast in the slow cooker.

• Set the cooker to low and cook the roast for about 5 - 6 hours or until the roast becomes tender. Remove roast from the slow cooker and place it on your cutting board.

• Let the roast cool slightly before shredding using two forks.

• Remove the fat floating on top in the slow cooker before transferring the cooking juices and veggies to a small saucepan. Let it boil on high heat.

• Gradually pour the cornstarch mixture into the saucepan with cooking juices. Continue cooking the juices for 3 - 4 four minutes or until the sauce becomes thick. Turn off the heat.

• Add the shredded beef, together with the vegetables and sauce, into the slow cooker and mix well. Heat thoroughly for 10 to 15 minutes.

• Place lettuce leaves on a serving platter.

• Enjoy the beef mixture served in lettuce leaves. You may also sprinkle with some green onions if you want.

Guacamole Salsa Bacon Burgers

Servings: 2

Nutrition per serving:

- Calories: 402
- Fat: 15 grams
- Carbs: 11 grams
- Protein: 32 grams

Ingredients

- 1 cup fresh salsa or Pico de Gallo
- ½ jalapeño chili pepper, seeded and finely chopped
- 1 medium ripe avocado, peeled, pitted mashed
- ½ pound lean ground beef
- ½ tablespoon fresh lime juice
- ¼ teaspoon salt
- ¼ teaspoon pepper
- 1 clove garlic, minced
- 1 tablespoons chopped fresh cilantro
- 1 tablespoons chopped green onions
- 2 butter lettuce leaves
- 3 slices no-sugar-added bacon

Instructions

- Line a rimmed baking sheet with foil while preheating your oven to 400°F.
- Place the bacon slices on the baking sheet, without overlapping, and bake them for up to 20 minutes or until they become crisp, whichever comes first. Once cooked, allow the bacon slices to cool and drain on paper towels before crumbling them.

• While waiting for the bacon slices to finish draining and cooling, mix 1/8 teaspoon salt, 1/8 teaspoon pepper, jalapenos, garlic, and ground beef in a mixing bowl. After you've crumbled the bacon pieces, gently mix them in the mixing bowl. Divide the mixture into two equal portions and form them into patties.

• Set up your grill and preheat it to medium (160°F). Place the burger patties on the grill for up to 12 - 16 minutes or until they are cooked to the desired doneness. Turn the patties after about 8 - 10 minutes of grilling.

• While waiting for the patties to cook, you can make guacamole. For this, combine the green onions, cilantro, the remaining 1/8 teaspoon of salt, 1/8 teaspoon pepper, lime juice, and avocado in another mixing bowl.

• Once the burger patties have been cooked, serve them in lettuce leaves and top with the guacamole mixture and fresh salsa.

Butter Garlic Pork Chops

Servings: 2

Nutrition per serving: Without asparagus

- Calories: 396
- Fat: 29 grams
- Carbs: 2 grams
- Protein: 29 grams

Ingredients

- ½ teaspoon Italian seasoning
- ¼ teaspoon pepper
- ½ teaspoon onion powder
- ¼ teaspoon salt
- 2 pork chops

Butter garlic sauce:

- ¼ cup chicken stock or broth or vegetable broth or any other broth
- ¼ cup heavy cream
- 1 ½ tablespoons butter
- 2 cloves garlic, minced
- ½ pound asparagus chopped (optional)
- ½ tablespoon lemon juice (optional)

Instructions

- Use onion powder, Italian seasoning, salt, and pepper to season both sides of your pork chops.

- In a skillet placed on high heat, melt the butter. Add garlic and stir for a few seconds or until fragrant.

- Throw the pork chops in and sear them for a couple of minutes on both sides.

- Drizzle the cream, lemon juice, and broth over the chops. Mix well by moving the meat around in the skillet. Allow the mixture to come to a boil before bringing down the heat to medium.

- Throw in the asparagus and let the mixture simmer for up to 10 minutes or until the sauce becomes thick, whichever comes first. If the chops are fully cooked before the sauce becomes thick, take out the chops from the mixture and set them aside until you finish the sauce.

Pulled Pork

Servings: 5

Nutrition per serving:

- Calories: 495
- Fat: 34 grams
- Carbs: 4 grams
- Protein: 43 grams

Ingredients

- 2 small bay leaves
- ½ teaspoon blackstrap molasses (optional for brown sugar flavor)
- ½ teaspoon ground mustard
- ½ teaspoon paprika
- ½ teaspoon salt
- 1/8 teaspoon stevia concentrated powder
- 1 chili pepper, chopped
- 1 tablespoon dry minced onion
- 1 tablespoon liquid smoke
- 1 teaspoon chili powder
- 1 teaspoon Worcestershire sauce
- 1 ½ tablespoons tomato paste
- 6 tablespoons white vinegar
- 2 pounds pork butt shoulder roast, trimmed of excess fat
- 3 garlic cloves chopped

Instructions

- Except for the pork roast and bay leaves, mix all the ingredients together in a bowl until you achieve a smooth textured mixture. If time allows, marinate the meat for several hours (overnight is best) in the mixture before cooking.

• In a large pot, place the pork roast and pour in the marinade/sauce mixture all over the pork roast. Throw the bay leaves in, together with ½ quart of water. Cover the pot and let the mixture come to a boil.

• Lower the flame and simmer for up to two hours or until the pork roast becomes tender enough to pull apart with a fork, whichever comes first. Turn the meat frequently while cooking.

• Once cooked, remove the pot from the heat and allow the meat to cool in the sauce. When cooled, remove the pork roast from the sauce and shred to pieces with two forks before setting aside.

• Heat the remaining sauce until it reduces to 2/3 of its original quantity. Add shredded pork to the sauce mixture. If you want, adjust the taste by seasoning with additional salt.

• Remove the bay leaves before serving/eating.

Garlic Herb Butter Pork Tenderloin

Servings: 4

Nutrition per serving:

- Calories: 237
- Fat: 15 grams
- Carbs: 1 grams
- Protein: 24 grams

Ingredients

- ½ tablespoon minced Italian herbs (mixture of rosemary, thyme, and sage)
- ½ teaspoon pepper
- ½ teaspoon salt
- 1 pound pork tenderloin
- 1 ½ tablespoons avocado oil
- 2 cloves garlic coarsely minced

For garlic Butter:

- ½ tablespoon chopped fresh parsley
- ¼ teaspoon onion powder
- 1/8 teaspoon garlic salt
- 1/8 cup melted unsalted butter

Instructions

- Pierce holes over the pork tenderloin while preheating your oven to 425° F. Make sure to pierce it all over the meat. Use minced herbs and sliced garlic to fill the holes. Sprinkle salt and pepper all over the meat.
- Pour oil into a cast-iron skillet and heat over medium-high heat.

• Place pork in the skillet, sear the pork for up to 3 minutes on each side or until they turn brown. Turn off the heat.

• Place the skillet in the oven and bake the pork for up to 25 minutes or until the thermometer inserted in the meat's thickest section registers 145° F.

• Take the skillet out of your oven and let it cool. While the meat is cooling, prepare the garlic butter by mixing all the garlic butter ingredients in a small mixing bowl.

• Cut the pork into 1-inch slices on a serving plate. Spoon the garlic butter mixture over it before enjoying.

Rosemary Garlic Pork

Servings: 4

Nutrition per serving:

- Calories: 237
- Fat: 15 grams
- Carbs: 2 grams
- Protein: 24 grams

Ingredients

- ½ pound Pork tenderloin, boneless, trimmed
- ½ tablespoon chopped fresh rosemary
- ½ teaspoon Italian seasoning
- ½ teaspoon sea salt
- ¼ teaspoon grated lemon zest
- 1/8 teaspoon black pepper
- 1 ½ tablespoons olive oil, divided into 1 tablespoon and ½ tablespoon
- 2 cloves garlic (crushed)

Instructions

- While heating your oven to 425° F, sprinkle both sides of the meat with salt and pepper.
- Mix together one tablespoon of olive oil, rosemary, garlic, lemon zest, and Italian seasoning in a small bowl. Brush all sides of the pork with this mixture.
- In a cast-iron skillet over medium-high heat, sear the pork tenderloin in the remaining ½ tablespoon olive oil for about 3 – 4 minutes, undisturbed until the bottom becomes brown. Turn the meat over and cook the other side undisturbed for 3 – 4 minutes or until brown. Turn off the heat.

• Put the skillet inside your heated oven and roast the pork for about 15 minutes or until the internal temperature of the pork reaches 145° F.

• Remove the tenderloin from the oven to rest for 5 minutes. Cut into slices and serve

Broccoli-Spinach Garlic Chicken

Servings: 2

Nutrition per serving:

- Calories: 360
- Fat: 23 grams
- Carbs: 7 grams
- Protein: 30 grams

Ingredients

- ½ pound chicken breasts cut into 1" pieces
- ½ teaspoon Italian seasoning
- ¼ cup shredded cheese mozzarella, cheddar or parmesan or favorite melting cheese
- ¼ cup tomatoes chopped
- 1/8 teaspoon crushed pepper optional
- 1 cup baby spinach
- 1 cup broccoli florets
- 1 tablespoon olive oil
- 2 cloves garlic minced
- 2 ounces cream cheese
- Salt and pepper to taste

Instructions

- Heat oil in a saucepan placed on medium-high heat. Sauté the chopped chicken breasts in the hot oil. Season it with salt, pepper, crushed red pepper, and Italian seasoning. Continue sautéing for up to 5 minutes or until the chicken is cooked and turns golden.
- Throw the garlic in and sauté for 1 minute more or until it becomes fragrant. Finally, mix the cream cheese, shredded cheese, spinach, broccoli, and tomato in and

continue cooking for up to 4 minutes more or until the broccoli is cooked and turns bright green.

• This dish goes well with cooked brown rice, cauliflower rice, or zucchini noodles.

Chicken Mozzarella

Servings: 2

Nutrition per serving:

- Calories: 309
- Fat: 9 grams
- Carbs: 9 grams
- Protein: 37 grams

Ingredients

- ½ fire-roasted bell pepper (fire-roasted capsicum), chopped
- ½ onion, chopped
- ½ tablespoon freshly chopped parsley, to garnish
- ½ tablespoon Italian seasoning
- ½ tablespoon olive oil
- ½ teaspoon paprika
- ½ teaspoon onion powder
- ½ can (from a 15 ounces can) crushed tomatoes or tomato puree (Passata)
- 1 tablespoon tomato paste, garlic, and herb-flavored if possible
- 6 tablespoons shredded mozzarella cheese
- 2 boneless skinless chicken breasts (5 ounces each)
- 2 cloves garlic, minced
- Pinch crushed red pepper flakes if desired
- Salt and pepper to taste

Instructions

- Set the oven to broil mode. Heat your broiler to medium heat and position the oven rack in the middle of your oven.

- Use salt, pepper, onion powder, paprika, and half of the Italian seasoning to flavor the chicken.

- In a pan or skillet on medium heat, cook the chicken in the oil for about 8 minutes per side or until both sides turn brown and are cooked through, whichever comes first. Set them aside on a plate when done.

- In the same pan or skillet, cook the onions for up to 4 minutes or until they become slightly soft. Make sure to scrape the cooked bits from the bottom of the pan before adding garlic. Cook for about 1 minute or until garlic turns aromatic.

- Throw in the fire-roasted pepper, tomato paste, crushed tomatoes, the remaining Italian seasoning, and crushed red pepper flakes. Mix the ingredients well and let the mixture simmer for a few minutes; stir occasionally, until it thickens. Turn off the heat.

- Place the chicken pieces in the sauce. Place about 2 – 3 tablespoons of mozzarella cheese on top of each chicken piece.

- Place the pan/skillet in the oven and broil for up to 2 minutes or until you see the cheese bubbling and turn brown at a few spots.

- Sprinkle parsley on top before serving. Enjoy!

Chili Aioli Buffalo Drumsticks

Servings: 2

Nutrition per serving:

- Calories: 570
- Fat: 42 grams
- Carbs: 4 grams
- Protein: 43 grams

Ingredients

For chicken and marinade:

- 1 tablespoon Tabasco
- ½ tablespoon tomato paste
- ½ teaspoon paprika powder
- ½ teaspoon salt
- 1 pound chicken drumsticks
- 1 tablespoon olive oil or coconut oil
- 1 tablespoon white wine vinegar

For chili aioli:

- 1 teaspoons chipotle powder
- 3 tablespoons mayonnaise or vegan mayonnaise
- 2 small garlic cloves, minced

For serving:

- 1 cup leafy greens

Instructions

- Prepare a baking sheet by lining it with parchment paper while preheating your oven to 365°F.
- Place the chicken pieces in a medium-sized mixing bowl or a Ziploc bag.

• Combine all the marinade ingredients in a mixing bowl and pour the mixture on the drumsticks, covering them completely. Seal the bag and set it aside to marinate for at least 10 minutes at room temperature.

• Remove the chicken pieces from the marinade and place them on the baking sheet to bake in the oven for about 40 minutes or until they become crispy and golden.

• While baking the chicken, combine all the chili aioli ingredients in a small mixing bowl and mix them thoroughly.

• Enjoy the drumsticks with the chili aioli dip.

Desserts and Snack Recipes

Choco Fat Bombs

Servings: 15

Nutrition per serving:

- Calories: 137
- Fat: 11 grams
- Carbs: 12 grams
- Protein: 2 grams

Ingredients

- ½ teaspoon pure vanilla extract
- 1 cup almond flour
- 4 ounces sugar-free chocolate chips
- 4.5 ounces dark chocolate chips
- ¼ cup butter softened
- ¼ teaspoon kosher salt
- 3 tablespoons Swerve confectioners' sugar or Erythritol sweetener

Instructions

- Prepare a baking sheet by lining it with parchment paper.
- Use a hand mixer to beat the butter in a mixing bowl until creamy. Add vanilla, salt, and sugar and continue mixing until all ingredients are thoroughly combined.
- Add almond flour in small quantities, mixing well on each addition of almond flour.
- Mix in the dark chocolate chips, and when done, cover the bowl with plastic wrap and keep it in the refrigerator for 10 to 15 minutes.

• Take the dough from the fridge and scoop out 15 equal portions. Shape into balls. Place them on the prepared baking sheet.

• Melt the sugar-free chocolate chips in a double boiler or microwave. If you are using a double boiler, make sure you are stirring until you achieve a smooth, melted consistency. If using a microwave oven, microwave the chips in a microwaveable dish in 30-second intervals. Stir during intervals to ensure smoothness.

• Dunk each of the chilled chocolate fat bombs in the melted chocolate mixture and return them to the baking sheet.

• Place the baking sheet in the freezer for up to 5 minutes or just enough to harden the chocolate covering.

Cranberry Blondies

Servings: 6

Nutrition per serving:

- Calories: 131
- Fat: 11 grams
- Net Carbs: 6 grams
- Protein: 3 grams

Ingredients

- ½ tablespoon ground flaxseeds
- 1 tablespoon coconut flour
- ½ cup blanched almond flour
- 1 tablespoon granulated sweetener of your choice like swerve or erythritol
- 2 tablespoons milk of your choice
- 2 tablespoons dried unsweetened cranberries
- ¼ cup almond butter
- ¼ teaspoon vanilla extract
- 1/8 cup sugar-free chocolate chips
- 1 ½ tablespoons water

Instructions

- Prepare a baking dish (6 x 6 inches) by lining it with parchment paper while preheating your oven to 350°F.
- To make flax egg, mix together ground flaxseeds with 1 ½ tablespoons of water. Let it rest for 15 minutes or until gel-like.
- Combine coconut flour, almond flour, and sweetener in a mixing bowl.
- Mix together flax egg, milk, vanilla extract, and almond butter in another bowl until smooth.

• Pour the mixture of wet ingredients into the bowl of flour mixture and stir until well incorporated.

• Add cranberries and most of the chocolate chips and fold gently. Spoon the mixture into the baking dish. Scatter remaining chocolate chips on top.

• Place the baking dish in the oven for 20 – 25 minutes or bake until golden brown around the edges. If you insert a toothpick in the center of the blondie and pull it out, it should not have any particles stuck on it. If you see any particles stuck on the toothpick, you need to bake for a few more minutes.

• Take out the baking dish and let it cool completely on your countertop, in the pan itself.

• Cut into six equal squares and serve.

Peanut Butter Cookies

Servings: 7

Nutrition per serving:

- Calories: 249
- Fat: 21 grams
- Carbs: 7 grams
- Protein: 21 grams

Ingredients

- 2 large eggs
- 1 teaspoon salt
- 1 ½ cups sugar-free peanut butter
- 1 teaspoon vanilla extract
- ½ cup butter
- 1 1/3 cups powdered erythritol

Instructions

- While preheating your oven to 360°F, mix all the ingredients in a big mixing bowl until thoroughly combined. Ensure the butter is softened before mixing.
- Divide the mixture into 14 equal portions and shape into balls.
- Keep them on a baking sheet, leaving a gap between them.
- Use a fork to flatten them.
- Bake the cookies in the heated oven for up to 20 minutes or until the cookies become slightly brown around the edges.
- Remove from the oven and let them cool on the baking sheet itself for about 20 minutes before enjoying.

No-Bake Choco-mint Bars

Servings: 5

Nutrition per serving:

- Calories: 123
- Fat: 11 grams
- Carbs: 7 grams
- Protein: 5 grams

Ingredients

For cookie bars:

- 1 tablespoon grass-fed ghee
- 1 tablespoon MitoSweet, or granulated erythritol/monk fruit blend
- 1 teaspoon organic chlorella powder
- 1 ½ cups shredded coconut
- 1 ½ teaspoons vanilla extract
- 2 – 3 drops food-grade peppermint essential oil
- 3 tablespoons collagen protein
- A pinch of salt

For chocolate drizzle:

- ½ tablespoon MitoSweet, or granulated erythritol/monk fruit blend, or 15 drops liquid stevia
- ½ teaspoon vanilla extract
- 1 tablespoon cacao powder
- 1 ½ tablespoons ghee or coconut oil, melted

Instructions

- Blend the coconut in a food processor at medium speed until it's finely chopped.
- Except for the collagen, blend in the remaining cookie bar ingredients until thoroughly combined.

- To avoid damaging the proteins, mix the collagen in at the lowest possible blender speed. It should be just combined, making sure not to over-mix.

- Line a small loaf pan with parchment paper. Spread the mixture into the loaf pan. Set aside in the freezer for a while to set.

- While waiting for the cookie bar mixture to set, mix all the chocolate drizzle ingredients in a small bowl until thoroughly combined.

- Once the mixture has set, remove it from the pan and cut slowly with a knife dipped or ran under hot water.

- Trickle the chocolate drizzle over the bars before freezing again for five more minutes.

Coco-Almond Sandies

Servings: 36

Nutrition per serving:

- Calories: 108
- Fat: 10 grams
- Carbs: 3 grams
- Protein: 2 grams

Ingredients

- 2 cups almond meal
- 2 cups unsweetened coconut
- 12 egg whites
- 2 tablespoons vanilla extract
- 1 teaspoon stevia powder, or to taste
- 1 teaspoon Himalayan sea salt
- 2/3 cup melted coconut oil
- 4 tablespoons water

Instructions

- While preheating your oven to 325°F, use parchment paper to line a baking sheet.
- In a big mixing bowl, mix the stevia powder, salt, vanilla extract, water, egg white, coconut oil, almond meal, and coconut. Let the mixture sit for about 10 minutes to let the coconut soften.
- Make 36 equal portions (about a tablespoon of the mixture) of the mixture and shape into balls. Place them on the baking sheet, leaving a gap between them. Use a fork to gently flatten them and prevent crumbling edges.

• Bake the cookies in the heated oven for up to 15 minutes or until the edges turn golden. Let them cool on the baking sheet for 1 minute before transferring to a wire rack to allow for complete cooling.

• Store in an airtight container.

7-Day Meal Plan

Day One:

Breakfast: Veggietatas

Lunch: Guacamole Salsa Bacon Burgers

Snack: Choco Fat Bombs

Dinner: Garlic Herb Butter Pork Tenderloin

Day Two:

Breakfast: Soft-Boiled Caprese

Lunch: Garlic Herb Butter Pork Tenderloin

Snack: No-Bake Choco-mint Bars

Dinner: Pulled Pork

Day Three:

Breakfast: Skillet Eggs and Chorizo

Lunch: Chipotle-Style Barbacoa

Snack: Choco Fat Bombs

Dinner: Chicken Mozzarella

Day Four:

Breakfast: Skillet Eggs and Chorizo

Lunch: Slow-cooked Shredded Beef in Lettuce Cups

Snack: Coco-Almond Sandies

Dinner: Rosemary Garlic Pork

Day Five:

Breakfast: Egg Salad

Lunch: Rosemary Garlic Pork

Snack: Peanut Butter Cookies

Dinner: Chili Aioli Buffalo Drumsticks

Day Six:

Breakfast: Bulletproof Coffee

Lunch: Broccoli-Spinach Garlic Chicken

Snack: No-Bake Choco-mint Bars

Dinner: Guacamole Salsa Bacon Burgers

Day Seven:

Breakfast: Veggietatas

Lunch: Broccoli-Spinach Garlic Chicken

Snack: Peanut Butter Cookies

Dinner: Garlic Herb Butter Pork Tenderloin

Chapter 8: Before You Dive In

You are now equipped with some handy and practical information to help you lose excess weight and keep it off using the endomorph diet. Let me share with you three practical but essential tips that can help you maximize your chances of achieving your weight loss goals.

The Right Goals

While your weight loss goals are personal, and no one can tell you whether it's right or wrong, it's essential to set your goals wisely. What do I mean by this?

Don't set goals that are too lofty or impractical. For example, you may want to lose 20 pounds of body fat. There's nothing wrong with that goal, but it would be unwise to try and accomplish it very quickly, say, in just one month. Why is it so?

First, you have already learned that a healthy weight loss rate is between one and two pounds per week because this maximizes the likelihood of mainly losing body fat instead of muscle mass and water. To lose 20 pounds of body fat given the ideal 2-pound weekly weight loss pace, it would take you at least ten weeks or roughly 2 1/2 months to do that.

One way to set your weight loss goals wisely is by avoiding unrealistic timelines. In situations like these, it's better to err on the side of caution and avoid significant disappointments.

Another way to set goals wisely is to break them down into smaller and easier subgoals. Going back to our 20-pound weight loss example, you can break it down into four or five smaller weight loss goals. Your first goal can be to lose 6 to 8 pounds during the first month, another 6 to 8 pounds in the second, and the last 4 to 8 pounds in the third month.

Breaking your primary goals into smaller ones gives you the benefit of higher morale. Smaller goals are easier to achieve, and the more you accomplish, the more encouraged you will get. Your mental and emotional momentum can help you sustain your efforts until your overall goal is achieved.

Finally, it's much better to focus on habit goals instead of results goals. To lose excess weight, you need to do certain things correctly and consistently. In the case of losing weight, it includes portion control, regular exercise, and calorie counting.

If you simply focus on achieving the weight loss, chances are high you'll stop doing the things that enabled you to succeed when you've lost your desired number of pounds. When that happens, you'll likely revert to the old habits that led to your weight gain, and over time, the weight you lost will return.

Another danger of focusing on results goals rather than habit goals is early discouragement. Suppose you don't accomplish the results in the timeframe you want. In that case, chances are you'll eventually stop doing the things that can help you lose weight because they will seem ineffective.

One challenge with weight loss strategies like the endomorph diet is that while they're scientifically proven to help people lose weight, they may work differently for different people. For some, they may be like diesel engines that take considerable time to warm up and achieve results from the same strategies as others. So, if you focus merely on the results and they don't come as quickly as you'd like them to, you may be tempted to stop altogether.

But if you focus on habit goals instead, like portion control, calorie counting, and regular exercise, you won't be easily discouraged when results don't come as quickly as you want them to. Then, you'll be able to consistently practice these long enough to where they become habits or automatic actions that require little or no willpower. At that point, these actions can deliver consistent results because, as a habit, you no longer need to think about them or stress over performing them regularly. This is the recipe for long-term success, which is losing weight and keeping it off for good.

Patience

As the saying goes, "Rome wasn't built in a day, but they were busy laying bricks by the hour." It means anything worth achieving doesn't happen overnight. It needs patience, consistency, and lots of baby steps.

You must avoid the temptation to speed up your weight loss process, especially if you're losing over two pounds each week. If you succumb to it, you'll likely lose more muscle mass than body fat and compromise your metabolism in the long run.

One way to exercise patience on this diet is by sticking to the appropriate caloric deficits. Don't give in to the temptation of cutting your daily calories by more than 15% of your TDEE. If you're losing over two pounds weekly despite limiting your caloric deficit to 15% at most, consider reducing the deficit until your weekly weight loss is between one and two pounds only.

Another way you can exercise patience is through regular exercise. Sometimes, the temptation to exercise too much by increasing the intensity, duration, or both can be irresistible. But you must resist because if you don't, you'll risk getting injured, burning out, or both.

Finally, don't apply everything you've learned perfectly in the beginning. This is especially true for the intermittent fasting part. There are two ways you can take baby steps.

One is by focusing on one fundamental principle first. That way, you'll be able to focus most of your attention and willpower on just one thing and prevent yourself from feeling overwhelmed. Once you've learned that principle and can apply it easily, add another one until you're able to apply everything.

Another way you can take baby steps is by partial completion. Take, for example, intermittent fasting. Instead of fasting for 16 hours every day at the start, why not start by skipping breakfast first if you choose the LeanGains intermittent fasting protocol and schedule your fasting hours starting early evening until around noon the next day. That way, you won't feel overwhelmed, and you can enjoy the benefit of progressing at your own pace.

It's All About You

No, I don't mean this in a selfish sense. By this, I mean you should never compare your progress – or lack thereof - to that of others. No two people are the same; each has its unique physiology, sets of circumstances, priorities, and available resources, among others. If you compare your weekly weight loss progress to that of your ectomorph friend, expect lots of discouragement because they will always have an easier time losing weight than you. Even if your friend is also an endomorph, comparing your progress to theirs is still unwise because both of you have different genetic makeups and personal circumstances that affect how fast or slow you're able to lose excess body fat.

Always remember that your weight loss goals are yours alone. Own it and don't let other people's developments dictate yours. Measure progress or lack thereof only against your own previous performance and results.

Conclusion

So, how that we're here and at the end of our journey together, I hope you've learned a lot of helpful information and are eager to start your own adventure immediately. After all, knowing is only half the battle. The real work comes with *application.*

Remember, applying what you have learned doesn't mean applying everything at once. Always remember what I wrote in the last chapter about patience. All significant accomplishments in life take time, and successfully losing excess body weight and keeping it off as an endomorph may be considered a significant life goal. Focus on developing the habits that will help you lose weight and keep it off, and eventually, results will follow.

Here's another book by Jena Ashley that you might like

References

Calorie Chart Meat + Fish + Seafood. (n.d.). Www.novafeel.com. Retrieved from http://www.novafeel.com/calories/calorie-chart-meat-fish.htm

Calvert, M. (n.d.). *4 Endomorph Diet Strategies to Accelerate Fat Loss.* STACK. Retrieved from https://www.stack.com/a/endomorph-diet

Carbohydrate and Calorie Content of Foods By Item. (n.d.). Www.momsteam.com. https://www.momsteam.com/nutrition/sports-nutrition-basics/nutritional-needs-guidelines/carbohydrate-and-calorie-content-of-foods

Cortes, A. J. A. (n.d.). *The Science of Somatotypes.* Elitefts. Retrieved from https://www.elitefts.com/education/training/bodybuilding/the-science-of-somatotypes/

Harvard Health Publishing. (2018, March 14). *Glycemic index for 60+ foods - Harvard Health.* Harvard Health; Harvard Health. https://www.health.harvard.edu/diseases-and-conditions/glycemic-index-and-glycemic-load-for-100-foods

Healthline: Medical information and health advice you can trust. (2000). Healthline.com. https://www.healthline.com/

Huizen, J. (2019, June 27). *What to know about the endomorph diet.* Medicalnewstoday.com; Medical News Today. https://www.medicalnewstoday.com/articles/325577

Somatotypes. (2019, October 7). TeachPE.com. https://www.teachpe.com/training-fitness/somatotypes

The Editors of Encyclopedia Britannica. (2015). Somatotype | physiology. In *Encyclopedia Britannica.* https://www.britannica.com/science/somatotype

The Story of the Endomorph: How to Work With What You Have. (n.d.). Breaking Muscle. Retrieved from https://breakingmuscle.com/healthy-eating/the-story-of-the-endomorph-how-to-work-with-what-you-have

Made in United States
North Haven, CT
01 March 2024

49407483R00078

Intergalactic Cell Phone

By Alan Trussell-Cullen

Illustrated by Lori Lambson

DOMINIE PRESS

Pearson Learning Group

Paperback ISBN 0-7685-1828-8
Printed in Singapore
   8 9 10 09

1-800-321-3106
www.pearsonlearning.com

Table of Contents

Chapter One
Orange Jelly

We were riding through the park on our bikes when Nat found it. Nat is Zane's twin sister. I'm Carlos, their friend.

The three of us went to a movie about aliens from Mars coming and taking over the Earth. Earthlings who didn't do what the Martians wanted were turned into orange jelly. Scary stuff!

Nat kept covering her eyes. Zane and I laughed every time someone got *jellied*, which only made Nat angry.

"Carlos! Zane! you guys are ruining the movie!" she complained.

"Yeah, right!" said Zane. "You're not watching it, anyway!"

That was why we weren't exactly riding our bikes together. Zane and I were riding in front of Nat and making jokes about how all that orange jelly was making us hungry!

Then we heard this a shout from Nat. She was looking at something on the ground.

"I think I found something," Nat said.

"Is it money?" I asked.

"Is it orange jelly?" asked Zane.

Nat ignored us both. She really had found something. We dropped our bikes and rushed back to look.

"Hey, that's a cell phone," said Zane.

"I guess so," said Nat. "But there aren't any numbers."

Instead of numbers, it had these funny characters on the buttons.

"Maybe it's a Japanese telephone and those are numbers in Japanese," I said.

"It doesn't look like Japanese writing," said Nat.

"So now you know Japanese?" I said.

"It's got a big text message screen," said Zane.

He was right. But somehow it didn't quite look like any text message screen we'd ever seen.

"Why don't we try calling someone?" Nat said. "Then we'll know if it's a real

phone."

"Who are we going to call?" I asked.

"I know," said Zane. "We can call our teacher."

"Oh, sure," I said. "She only kept you after school every day of the week! I think you're the last person she'd want to hear from!"

But Nat was already dialing. She was pushing the buttons as if they were regular numbers. "I'm calling my friend Tina," she said.

She put the phone to her ear and listened. Suddenly, her eyes started to get bigger and bigger.

"What's the matter?" we asked. "Is that Tina?"

Nat was having trouble speaking. "There's a voice. A sort of a voice. It's sort of..."

She took the phone away from her ear.

That's when we all saw the screen. It had been blank before. But now it was glowing green, and in the middle was the face of a very strange creature—and it seemed to be talking.

"Zak zik rok rak? Zak zik rok rak?"

We all gasped. It certainly wasn't Tina!

None of us wanted to say anything, but Nat finally said, "I think we've dialed some creature from outer space!"

"Oh, right," I said. "Outer space, sure."

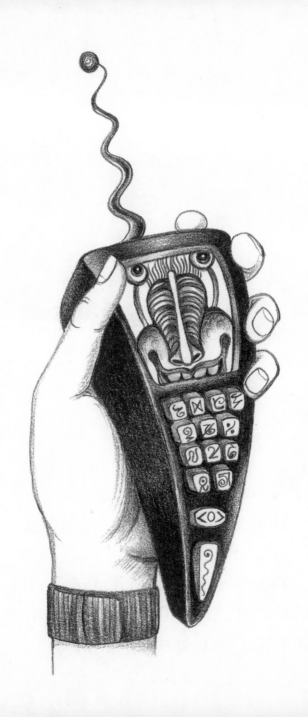

11

Chapter Two
The Flying Saucer

"**A**nswer it!" Zane said.

"How can I answer it?" said Nat.
"I don't speak *Zak zik!*"

"*Zak zik!*" said the creature on the
phone. "Wait, earth-thing! I switch
translator on and try earth-thing

language!"

"Earth-thing?" asked Zane.

"I think he means *earthling*," I said. I didn't believe this "creature" was really from outer space, but I played along.

"My name is Zeb, and I live on the planet Zakroid," the creature said.

"Hi, Zeb!" we all shouted.

"I'm Nat," said Nat. "And this is Zane and Carlos."

Then something weird happened. The funny creature on the screen began to change shape. Soon it looked like a regular kid from Earth.

"How did you do that?" asked Zane.

"Computer graphics," I muttered. But Zane shushed me.

"We Zakroidians have control of our own DNA," Zeb said. "It means we can change ourselves to look like anything we like. That is why no one recognized me and my parents when we visited your planet."

"When was that?" asked Nat.

"A week ago, your time," Zeb said.

"The flying saucer!" said Zane. "Remember? People said they thought they had seen a flying saucer landing. And everyone's TV went funny, and all

the street lights came on in the middle of the day."

"No one really believes it was a flying saucer," I said.

"Yes, well, sometimes our rockets do that," said Zeb.

"They work on micro-light waves, you see, and sometimes they can upset communication signals. But I am really glad you found my ICP."

"Your what?" Nat asked.

"Sorry," said Zeb, "ICP means Intergalactic Cell Phone. I must have dropped it when I was learning to use a skateboard. I will be in big trouble when my parents find out I left it behind. I will probably get a really big time-out."

"How long is a big time-out on Zakroid?" asked Zane.

"You *would* ask that," said Nat.

"You're the time-out king."

"Two years," said Zeb.

"Two years' time-out?" shrieked Zane. "Man, they're tough on your planet!"

"Is there any way we can get your ICP back to you?" asked Nat.

"Yeah, send it through mail," I said to Zane with a snicker.

"You could bring it to me, if you like," Zeb said.

That startled us all. I was probably the most startled.

"You're joking, right?" asked Nat.

"Oh, no," said Zeb. "Your time scale is different from ours. It would take me years to come back to your planet. But I can change your DNA using the ICP. Then I can transport you here to Zakroid in twenty minutes, your time."

I nearly fell over!

"Seriously?" asked Nat.

"Let's do it!" said Zane.

I was uneasy about the whole thing, but I still didn't really believe it. Computers could explain why we were seeing such weird things on the cell phone. But what would happen if we really were transported to another planet?

Chapter Three
A Time-Out

My disbelief didn't last much longer.

It's a weird experience being beamed millions of miles across space to another planet. First, you feel like you've got pins and needles all over your body. Then you feel like you're being squeezed into a very tiny bubble. The next moment, we opened our eyes, and there we were—on Zakroid!

"Welcome to my planet!" said a strange green creature.

"Are you Zeb?" said Zane. "But you're all green and... I mean... You looked different over the phone."

"This is what I look like when my DNA is Zakroid," said Zeb. "I have changed your DNA to Zakroid, too. Have you had a look at yourselves yet?"

We all turned to look at each other.

"Aaack!" we all gasped. Not only had we all turned completely green from the top of what used to be our heads to what now seemed to be our toes, but we were all sort of a round, pear shape. We didn't really have necks anymore—just bodies that sort of got smaller at the top. And

our arms sort of came out of our bodies
at about the same place as our legs. The
worst thing was our hair. It stuck straight
up in the air as if we were frightened by
something.

"Man, do you two look weird!"
laughed Zane.

"Speak for yourself, you talking
avocado!" said Nat.

"Have a look around while you're
here," said Zeb. "In fact, why don't you
come to school with me for the day? I'll
pretend you're my cousins from the other
side of Zakroid."

"But we can't spend a whole day here.
Our parents will get really worried!" said
Nat.

Zeb laughed. "A day in our time is
about half a minute in your time."

School on Zakroid was great fun for

Nat and me. Zane, of course, got into trouble—but more about that later.

The school looked like a whole lot of pumpkins stacked on top of each other. Each pumpkin was a classroom. The classrooms were completely round, but they had a plastic elevator that went up through the middle. You moved to another classroom by taking the plastic elevator.

They didn't have notebooks or pens and paper. Instead, they tapped away all day on their ICPs.

Their teachers were very strict. If you wanted to ask a question, instead of putting up your hand, you had to make a kind of "raspberry" noise. The teachers made raspberry noises when they were asking the children questions, too. It sounded very rude! It didn't take Zane

long to start giggling. Zeb looked horrified.

"Zane!" whispered Zeb. "You don't giggle on Zakroid. People think it is very bad manners."

Of course, this only made Zane giggle all the more. Suddenly, he found the teacher standing in front of him and pointing to the time-out room. You'll never guess how long of a time-out he had! Six whole weeks! It's just as well Zane doesn't live on Zakroid!

During recess, Zeb, Nat, and I took the plastic elevator down to the time-out room. It was down at the bottom of the bottom pumpkin. Zane was sitting on a stool, staring at a chart showing the chemical structure of Zakroidian DNA and looking very sorry for himself.

"Six weeks!" he shrieked when he saw

us. "I'll never get back to Earth! Mom and Dad will be furious!"

"Calm down," said Nat. "It's six weeks Zakroidian time! We'll wait for you!"

"And anyway," said Zeb. "Here on Zakroid, a school day takes five months. You will be out of here by lunchtime."

"I want to go home," said Zane.

"But we're having fun!" said Nat. "After recess, we're going to see a movie. It looks like that's how they learn math here."

"I want to go home now!" said Zane.

Nat put an arm around her twin and gave him a hug, kind of. "We're only teasing," she said. "Zeb says we can go home whenever we want."

"Can you beam us back from down here?" I asked.

"No problem!" said Zeb. "Or as you

earth-things say, 'A piece of cookie!' "

"Cake," I said.

Zeb began to push the buttons on his ICP. Once again, we felt that pins-and-needles feeling. Then came a feeling that we were toothpaste being pushed back into the tube! And suddenly, there we were, standing in the park beside our bikes. We were a little stunned at first. People walking by kept looking at us. One woman even giggled at us.

"Don't you know it's very rude to giggle?" said Zane. "They'll give you a time-out for months and months!"

The woman stopped giggling and hurried away.

We looked at each other. We seemed to be our normal selves again—except for our hair, which stuck straight up. We all tried to push it down, but it just popped

straight up again. We looked at our watches. We'd spent a whole month on Zakroid, but according to our watches, we had only been away for half an hour.

"We should get home before we get into trouble for being late!" said Zane. "I don't want any more time-outs!"

"Last one home is orange jelly!" said Nat. And we pedaled off at top speed.